The Major Plays of Nikolai Erdman

Russian Theatre Archive

A series of books edited by John Freedman (Moscow), Leon Gitelman (St Petersburg) and Anatoly Smeliansky (Moscow)

This book is part of a series. The publisher will accept continuation orders which may be cancelled at any time and which provide for automatic billing and shipping of each title in the series upon publication. Please write for details.

The Major Plays of Nikolai Erdman

The Warrant and *The Suicide*

translated and edited by
John Freedman

harwood academic publishers
Australia • Austria • China • France • Germany • India • Japan
Luxembourg • Malaysia • Netherlands • Russia • Singapore
Switzerland • Thailand • United Kingdom • United States

Applications for licences to perform the plays should be addressed to the translator, c/o Harwood Academic Publishers GmbH, 3 Boulevard Royal, L-2449 Luxembourg.

Cover illustration: drawing of Nikolai Erdman by Boris Erdman, 1922.

British Library Cataloguing in Publication Data

Erdman, Nikolai
    Major Plays of Nikolai Erdman:
    "Warrant" and "Suicide". – (Russian Theatre
    Archive, ISSN 1068-8161; Vol. 1)
    I. Title   II. Freedman, John   III. Series
    891.7242

ISBN 3-7186-5582-9 (hardback)
ISBN 3-7186-5583-7 (paperback)

CONTENTS

LIST OF PLATES
(Between pp. 84 and 85)

1. Nikolai Erdman, mid-1920s.
2. Vsevolod Meyerhold, Nikolai Erdman, Vladimir Mayakovsky, 1928–9.
3. Vsevolod Meyerhold, Vladimir Mayakovsky, Nikolai Erdman, 1928–9.
4. Nikolai Erdman and the actor Boris Chirkov, 1940s.
5. Nikolai Erdman (third from right) at the funeral of Sergei Yesenin, December 1925. On the left, Vsevolod Meyerhold and his wife, the actress Zinaida Raikh, who was formerly married to Yesenin.
6. Nikolai Erdman with his father Robert Erdman, 1946.
7. Nikolai Erdman, 1950(?).
8. Nikolai Erdman (right) and director Konstantin Yudin (centre) with an unknown stable hand during the filming of *Courageous People*, 1950.
9. Official portrait of Nikolai Erdman, 1951, taken in connection with his receiving the Stalin Prize with Mikhail Volpin for their script to the film *Courageous People*.
10. Nikolai Erdman, early 1960s.
11. Nikolai Erdman, 1965.
12. A scene from *The Warrant* at the Renaissance Theater, Berlin, 1927. Photo: Harvard College Library.
13. A scene from *The Suicide* at the Trinity Square Repertory, Providence, R.I., 1980. Photo: Constance Brown.
14. Derek Meader (Viktor) and Richard Jenkins (Semyon) in *The Suicide* at the Trinity Square Repertory, Providence, R.I., 1980. Photo: Constance Brown.
15. Veniamin Smekhov (Aristarkh) and Filipp Antipov (Semyon) in *The Suicide* at the Taganka Theater, Moscow, 1991.
16. Yury Smirnov (Kalabushkin), Mariya Politseimako (Mariya) and Veniamin Smekhov (Aristarkh) at the Taganka Theater, Moscow 1991.

INTRODUCTION TO THE SERIES

The Russian Theatre Archive makes available in English the best avant-garde plays, from the pre-Revolutionary period to the present day. It features monographs on major playwrights and theatre directors, introductions to previously unknown works, and studies of the main artistic groups and periods.

Plays are presented in performing edition translations, including (where appropriate) musical scores, and instructions for music and dance. Whenever possible the translated texts will be accompanied by videotapes of performances of plays in the original language.

Nikolai Erdman in the late 1920s.

INTRODUCTION

Nikolai Erdman is best known in the West for his second full-length play, *The Suicide*, called "a work of genius" by Konstantin Stanislavsky and "empty and even harmful" by the self-proclaimed dilettante in theatrical matters, Joseph Stalin. As is now well known, it was the latter's opinion which dictated that *The Suicide*, written in the late 1920s, would gather dust in archives and personal libraries for forty years before it could be performed. Following its world première on March 28, 1969 in Göteborg, Sweden, *The Suicide* was staged throughout the 1970s and 1980s by a staggering number of theaters in Germany, Switzerland, Holland, Finland, France, Belgium (in Flemish), Italy, South Africa (in Afrikaans), Canada, England and the United States.

Less known is Erdman's first major work, *The Warrant*, Vsevolod Meyerhold's staging of which went down in history as one of that director's most successful. Touted by a long line of cultural luminaries as a new Gogol, a brilliant stylist and the founder of a new drama, Erdman saw *The Warrant* become one of the most controversial and most frequently-staged plays in the Soviet Union. After its première at the Meyerhold Theater on April 20, 1925, it was produced in over thirty theaters and clubs in the 1925–1926 season alone. The following season, that number grew to forty. It was translated into German in 1926 and performed the following year at the Renaissance Theater in Berlin. But, due to a confluence of complications which arose at about that time — Stalin's rise to power, the negative reputation garnered by *The Suicide* and Erdman's censorship trouble with other works — *The Warrant* soon faded from view. Aside from a short-lived production at the Moscow Film Actors' Theater during the Thaw in 1956, it was relegated to the status of a footnote in Russian theater history. It resurfaced, this time in the West, only after the discovery of *The Suicide*. Although it enjoyed modest success in Europe, especially in Germany, *The Warrant* has been produced in English only a handful of times.

Erdman was born on November 16, 1900[1] in Moscow, the son of a Baltic-German father and a Russian mother. He made his literary debut in 1919 as a poet, publishing a few unusually well-crafted poems in obscure maga-

---

[1] Erdman's birth date is often given erroneously as 1902 due to a typographical error in the 1934 edition of the *Great Soviet Encyclopedia*. Pleased at having gained two years, Erdman never corrected the error.

zines connected with the group of poets who called themselves the Imagists and who were led by the bad boy of Russian poetry, Sergei Yesenin.

It wasn't long, however, before the young poet was drawn to the theater. After a stint in the Red Army—where he served as a scribe and did his best to avoid the line of fire that raged as the civil war neared an end — he began writing humorous topical songs and skits for a host of Moscow's most popular nightclub entertainers. In March 1922 he was invited by his Imagist friend Vadim Shershenevich to compose rehearsal texts for the Experimental-Heroic Theater. Just three months later, his adaptation of an operetta by Jacques Offenbach, entitled *Madame Archduke*, premièred at Mastfor, an experimental theater run by the legendary director Nikolai Foregger.[2] In the next two and a half years, Erdman produced some twenty short-to-medium-length plays or sketches which were staged at several of Moscow's most fashionable cabarets and small theaters.[3]

His first major success came when he was asked to co-author the first play for the newly-founded Moscow Theater of Satire. Together with David Gutman, Vladimir Mass and Viktor Tipot, he wrote a revue in five acts entitled *Moscow from a Point of View*. Premièring on October 1, 1924, it quickly became one of the hottest tickets in Moscow and exerted a significant influence on scores of other directors and playwrights, Vladimir Mayakovsky included.

Erdman was then engaged by the Vakhtangov Theater to write a modern adaptation of *Lev Gurych Sinichkin*, the classic Russian vaudeville by Dmitry Lensky. Its première on December 16, 1924, confirmed that a new playwright of unusual talent had emerged. *Sinichkin* remained in repertory at the Vakhtangov for ten years, being dropped only after Erdman was exiled to Siberia.

What few knew at the end of 1924, however, was that Erdman had already been noticed. And the observant eye belonged to none other than Vsevolod Meyerhold. The fact is that Erdman had already been putting the finishing touches on a new full-length play as early as January of 1924. Perhaps through the intercession of Erdman's good friend Vladimir Mass, who worked for a time as Meyerhold's literary director at the Theater of the Revolution, it came to the attention of Meyerhold himself. The Master, as he was called by those who worked for him, wasted no time in passing judgement, and the theater signed a contract with Erdman for *The Warrant* in the spring of 1924. When Meyerhold moved on to create his own theater that fall, he took *The Warrant* with him, making it the second première at the new

---

[2] *Madame Archduke* may have been based on Offenbach's *La Grande Duchesse de Gerolstein*, although we cannot know for sure, since no text has survived.

[3] Translations of some of these and other sketches can be found in *A Meeting About Laughter: Sketches, Interludes and Theatrical Parodies by Nikolai Erdman with Vladimir Mass and Others*, which is the second volume of the *Russian Theatre Archive* series.

Meyerhold Theater, following Alexei Faiko's *The Teacher Bubus*, which opened in January of 1925.

It is hardly exaggerating to say that Erdman became an overnight sensation. But what is more interesting is the difficulty people encountered in describing his style. Meyerhold's claim that he was poised to carry on the great tradition of Russian comic drama, established by Nikolai Gogol and Alexander Sukhovo-Kobylin, was picked up and repeated frequently. Anatoly Lunacharsky, the commissar of education, lavished praise on Erdman, saying, "Erdman derives from Chekhov, he is a pupil of Chekhov."[4] Pavel Markov, one of Russia's finest theater critics and scholars of the 20th century, was not satisfied by such formulaic approaches. He called *The Warrant* "the beginning of a new theater."[5]

Expanding on his views at a public discussion just a few weeks after the play's première, Markov asked, "Where did this play come from? By the very fact alone that it arose from the restoration of old theatrical forms we can oppose it profoundly to all other attempts of contemporary drama. It arises from that theater which for seven years has been breaking down theatrical forms . . . . Now Erdman with his *Warrant* is building a new comedy out of broken dramaturgical forms. Whatever traditions we may try to find for this playwright — here we are intentionally and stubbornly seeking resonances in this play from Gogol and Sukhovo-Kobylin — I believe that the significance of this play is not to be found in resonances of Gogol and Sukhovo-Kobylin, or in resonances of an old-style dramaturgy. When one talks about [*The Warrant*], one must think not only about the tradition which is fundamental to it — as obvious and clear-cut as that may be — but about the new possibilities that are provided by this play . . . ."[6]

Erdman himself wasted no time in preparing to develop those new possibilities. Immediately after the première of *The Warrant*, he signed a contract with Meyerhold for a new play, and, on May 22, 1925, the Moscow Art Theater announced that Erdman had agreed to write a new play for them for the 1925–1926 season. But the new play turned out to be a long time in coming. While there is reason to believe that parts of *The Suicide* were composed as early as the winter of 1925, the first surviving manuscripts date to late 1926. They are scribbled on the backsides of the script Erdman was writing for a film comedy, *Mitya*, also featuring a character who cannot decide whether or not to kill himself.

By the time Meyerhold began imploring Erdman in 1928 to deliver *The Suicide* as soon as possible for production at the Meyerhold Theater, the at-

[4] A. V. Lunacharsky, "V. G. Korolenko. A. P. Chekhov," in *Ocherki po istorii russkoi literatury* (Moscow: Khudozhestvennaya literatura, 1976), 425.
[5] Quoted in John Freedman, *Silence's Roar: The Life and Drama of Nikolai Erdman* (Oakville, Canada: Mosaic Press, 1992), 88.
[6] Quoted in *Silence's Roar: The Life and Drama of Nikolai Erdman*, 71–72.

mosphere in the country had changed drastically. Erdman's old friend Sergei Yesenin had either committed suicide or had been murdered by the secret police; the rigorously ideological Russian Association of Proletarian Writers (RAPP) had seized almost total control in the sphere of literature; Lev Kamenev had become one of the first of Lenin's old guard to be expelled from the Communist Party; and Joseph Stalin had solidified his position as the most powerful man in the Soviet Union.

Whether he knew it or not (it would appear that he did), Erdman's career was already on the wane. While work on *The Suicide* progressed slowly throughout 1928, Erdman entered into a partnership with Vladimir Mass that lasted until both were arrested in 1933. They wrote a series of satirical music hall revues, all of which were subjected to wicked attacks from censors and in the press, and many of which were banned. *The Suicide* was probably only completed in 1930, when readings of it took place in April at the Moscow Art Theater and in September at the Vakhtangov Theater. It was banned for the first time on September 25, 1930.

With the help of Maxim Gorky, Stanislavsky succeeded in getting Stalin to overturn the ban in November 1931, giving *The Suicide* a momentary second life and unleashing a series of vicious responses from those who did not like Erdman or his play. Stanislavsky's chosen director, Vasily Sakhnovsky, led rehearsals from late December until May 1932, although he never got further than the first two acts. Just eleven days before the Art Theater gave up on *The Suicide*, Meyerhold finally set to work on it. But his hopes of including the play in repertory were dashed after he gave a closed showing of the play's final three acts to a contingent of high-placed bureaucrats in October. Lazar Kaganovich, one of Stalin's right-hand men and the country's top censor, nonchalantly told Meyerhold afterwards, "There's no need to work on this play."[7]

A year later, on October 10, 1933, Erdman was arrested together with Vladimir Mass in the resort town of Gagra on the Black Sea where they were taking part in the filming of the movie *Jolly Fellows*, for which they had written the script. The official explanation was that they had written a series of anti-Soviet fables, but it is clear now that the real culprit was *The Suicide*. Mass, as Erdman's close associate and frequent co-author, probably fell victim to the authorities' need for a less controversial pretext to put an end to Erdman's career.

After spending about a week in prison in Moscow at the Lubyanka headquarters of the NKVD — the secret police — Erdman was shipped off hurriedly to the Siberian town of Yeniseisk where he spent his first year of exile. The last two years of his three-year sentence were spent in Tomsk.

---

[7] Quoted in Yury Zayats, "Ya prishyol k tyagostnomu ubezhdeniyu, chto ne nuzhen" [I Had Come to the Painful Conclusion that I Wasn't Needed], in *Meierkhol'dovsky sbornik*, issue 1, vol. II (Moscow: Tvorchesky tsentr imeni Vs. Meierkhol'da, 1992), 125.

During these years he worked sporadically on a new comedy, *The Hypnotist*. But it soon became evident that his days as a serious playwright were over. He was not fated to complete this play. Just three months after Erdman's exile ended, Meyerhold's theater was closed, one of the justifications for which was the director's previous attempts to stage *The Suicide*. Erdman's talent for comedy was not only "unnecessary," it had become dangerous.

From 1937 until his death in 1970, Erdman led a quiet, if uneasy, existence writing filmscripts, stage adaptations, libretti for operettas and sketches for stand-up comics. Almost everything he produced bore the distinct stamp of his unique talent, but he was always the first to admit it was nothing more than a means to earning a living. After Stalin's death in 1953, when scores of "forgotten" names were rehabilitated, Erdman was passed over in near total silence. A plan to publish *The Warrant* in 1954 was abandoned in the early stages, while the play's revival in 1956 was closed down just a few months after it opened. Two plans to stage *The Suicide* in 1956 — at the Vakhtangov Theater and the Mayakovsky Theater — never got beyond preliminary discussions. In 1965, Yury Lyubimov worked on the play for a month at the Taganka Theater before the Soviet Minister of Culture told him not to waste his time any further. In 1968, *The Suicide* was already typeset and corrected for publication in the December issue of *Theater*, but a directive came from above at the last minute to pull it out.

Erdman learned that *The Suicide* had survived the efforts to condemn it to oblivion just a year and a half before his death, when it received its world première in Sweden. What he didn't know was that another production had been fast approaching dress rehearsals even in the spring of 1968. The city was Prague and the timing couldn't have been worse. When Soviet tanks rolled into the Czechoslovakian capital, the première of *The Suicide* was not the only thing to be sacrificed.[8] However, the text quickly found its way westward, and so it was that the Swedish première directed by Johan Falck at the Stadsteatern was the event which finally sparked intense worldwide interest in Erdman's work.

The Suicide first appeared in English in 1976, when Alan Richardson staged it at the Theatre Compact in Toronto, Canada. That was followed by the U.S. première in 1978 at the New York Farce Company, under the direction of Robert O'Rourke. But it was Ron Daniels, with the Royal Shakespeare Company in Stratford-upon-Avon, and Jonas Jurasas, with the Trinity Square Repertory Company in Providence, Rhode Island, whose productions in 1979 and 1980, respectively, caused what can be called the English Erdman boom in the early 1980s.

---

[8] This information was first made public by Andrea Gotzes in her article "Postanovki p'es N. Erdmana na nemetskom yazyke v zerkale kritiki" [German-Language Stagings of N. Erdman's Plays in the Mirror of Criticism], *Sovremennaya dramaturgiya*, No. 5 (1989), 244.

Daniels's original work at The Other Place was transferred with equal success in 1980 to the RSC's small London venue, The Warehouse, and then was expanded in 1981 to suit the RSC's main stage at The Aldwych. All three garnered international acclaim. Jurasas's production at Trinity Square brought him an invitation to mount the play in October 1980 at the old ANTA Theater, where Derek Jacobi made his Broadway debut in the role of Semyon. Simultaneously, several of the best regional theaters in the United States, including the Arena Stage in Washington, D.C., the Goodman Theater in Chicago and the Yale Repertory Company, staged their own versions.

After an aborted attempt to stage *The Suicide* in Moscow in 1982 (the Moscow Theater of Satire performed it six times before it was banned), Erdman's plays finally began reappearing in his homeland in 1987. By 1989, *The Suicide* was the fourth most-staged play in the Soviet Union.[9]

But even in success, Erdman's plays were still haunted by the political specter which hung over him for most of his adult life. In the West, one of the stock phrases repeated in almost every review of *The Suicide* was, "It's no wonder this play was banned." Informed by the Cold War mentality, Western audiences were titillated most by the image of a playwright who had been so "daring." Similarly, when they finally got a chance, Soviet audiences rushed to the theaters to see a politically charged play by a legendary "dissident." But as the Soviet Union was rocked by an unending stream of sensational historical disclosures and then finally collapsed altogether, the "politics" of Erdman's drama were naturally unable to compete with what was transpiring in the real world. By 1993, in the newly independent Russia, *The Warrant* and *The Suicide* had acquired an awkward reputation as indecipherable hieroglyphs. Few doubted their brilliance, but no one knew what to do with them.

The end of the Cold War, however, and the end of the artificial separation of Russian culture into "official" and "dissident," or "Soviet" and "émigré," afford a new luxury. For the first time, Erdman's plays can be staged, performed and evaluated as they were intended: as works of dramatic art. What has to be understood now is, just what was Nikolai Erdman up to?

We can start by stating what he was not up to. The purpose of *The Warrant* was no more to ridicule the petty bourgeoisie than the purpose of *The Suicide* was to attack the Soviet Union. Like any talented writer, Erdman's goal was to create an artistic universe which, naturally, would enter into dialogue with the real world he inhabited, but which ultimately would func-

---

[9] Vitaly Dmitrievsky, "Repertuar perestroiki" [The Repertory of Perestroika], *Sovremennaya dramaturgiya*, No. 3 (1991), 134. For glimpses at some of these productions, see John Freedman, "Three Soviet *Suicides*," *Soviet and East European Performance*, No. 2 (1991), 37–45; and Scott T. Cummings, "*The Suicide* Comes 'Full Circle' in Cleveland," *Slavic and East European Performance*, Nos. 2/3 (1992), 44–48.

tion according to its own laws.[10] No other proof of this is needed than to note the two predominant approaches to *The Warrant* and *The Suicide*. Both were praised or criticized, at times, for being attacks on what once were called "former people," representatives of the tsarist bourgeoisie, while both were praised or criticized, at other times, for providing them with an eloquent defense. The ambiguity of the plays' alleged "political" orientation is a self-contained answer to every question it poses. The point is not whom the plays attack or defend, but what they say about the human experience and how they go about saying it. That is what Pavel Markov was driving at when he called *The Warrant* "the beginning of a new theater." Had Erdman been free to continue his experiments — what he once called "an extremely difficult technical and formal task"[11] — he might have made our own task in understanding them easier. History, however, dictated otherwise and now we are left to make do with what we have.

Two enigmatic observations by Meyerhold and Stanislavsky shed a ray of light on Erdman's unique dramatic method. During rehearsals of *The Warrant*, Meyerhold cautioned the actors against speaking their lines too loudly, telling them to penetrate the play's meaning through its "secret passageways . . . . The text," he continued, "is so constructed as to be very easy to approach."[12] Stanislavsky also picked up on what Meyerhold called Erdman's "secret passageways," although he was baffled by them. Recalling one of Erdman's famous readings of *The Suicide*, Stanislavsky wrote Erdman's "reading is absolutely marvelous and is very instructive for a director. There is some new quality hidden in his manner of speech which I could not quite decipher. I laughed so hard that I had to ask him to take an extended break or my heart would have given out."[13]

Erdman's "manner of speech," of course, was not merely the legendary, dead-pan tone in which he read. More importantly, it was his total subordination, as *performer* of his own play, to the unusual structure of language, characterization and situation that marks his major works. The poet-turned-playwright was working towards an innovative style of drama that moved beyond the traditional character- and plot-oriented theater text. His was a holistic approach in which the central themes of the play are suggested or inferred rather than stated or demonstrated.

---

[10] For an excellent account about how *The Warrant* reflected and parodied contemporary political demands, which, in their own turn, exerted a distorting influence on the reactions to the play, see Mikhail Smolyanitsky, "Postanovki p'esy N. R. Erdmana 'Mandat' v teatre imeni Vs. Meierkhol'da (epizod iz obshchestvennogo soznaniya serediny 20-kh gg [The Staging of N. R. Erdman's 'The Warrant' at the Meyerhold Theater (an example of the social consciousness of the mid-'20s)], *Zerkalo istorii* (Moscow: Rossiisky gosudarstvenny gumanitarny universitet, 1992), 109–122.
[11] Quoted in Zayats, "Ya prishyol k tyagostnomu ubezhdeniyu, chto ne nuzhen," 125.
[12] Quoted in *Silence's Roar: The Life and Drama of Nikolai Erdman*, 60–61.
[13] Quoted in *Silence's Roar: The Life and Drama of Nikolai Erdman*, 158–159.

The Warrant comprises a melange of styles that includes the 19th-century European vaudeville, traditional Russian "serious comedy," the slapstick of cabaret humor and the grotesque of the tragi-comic farce. On the surface, the action revolves around the wacky adventures of two families, the Gulyachkins and the Smetaniches. Before the cataclysms of the revolution deprived them of their livelihood, and more importantly, of their sense of identity, the former were petty merchants, while the latter were wealthy landowners and industrialists. The play progresses as these two displaced families struggle to find a place for themselves in alien and hostile surroundings. Each exists under the illusion that the other can help them do that, and, as is often the case in comedy, marriage is the means.

Deprived of a source of income, Nadezhda Gulyachkina wants to marry off her daughter Varvara to Valerian, the son of the still-wealthy Olimp Smetanich. As a way to entice the millionaire, Nadezhda tells him that her son Pavel is a communist who can provide protection should he ever need it. That is just the kind of "dowry" Olimp is looking for. At first, Pavel balks at his mother's insistence that he join the Communist Party. But when he realizes that this step will endow him with a sense of power, he composes a phony warrant (stating that he lives in the building in which he lives) and takes to bullying everyone around him. Everyone's plans are turned inside out when a friend of Nadezhda asks her to caretake a dress which once belonged to the empress. A series of comic interludes involving the dress leads the Smetaniches to believe that Nastya, the Gulyachkin's cook, is the tsaritsa Anastasiya Nikolayevna, and, encouraged by the reappearance in Moscow of a member of the royal family, they begin making plans for the fall of communist rule. More comic misunderstandings cause Nastya to think she has been offered Smetanich's son's hand in marriage and she accepts (having already accepted a marriage proposal from Ivan Shironkin, the Gulyachkin's boarder). Thus, three weddings involving three people are arranged in the span of two days. When all of the confusion and deceptions are cleared away in the riotous final scenes, the stunned characters are caught in a no man's land, a breach between destruction and self-discovery.

Despite the thick layer of slapstick comedy, Erdman's intent was anything but merely to fill his play with wisecracks. In fact, what some have called a contrived plot is the result of a complex dramatic structure which, no less than characterization and action, carries the kernel of the play's themes. The primary building block in Erdman's drama is the word. But, instead of being an expressive tool and a means of communication, it usually serves to confuse or to mislead. The crazy adventures of this strange dramatic world are the inevitable consequences of carelessly uttered or improperly understood words. Both Valerian and Nastya, for instance, twice find themselves getting engaged to be married, not so much because they want to, but because the dialogue dictates it.

Erdman reversed the relationship that is commonly assumed to exist between people and the language they use. In his drama, as is often the case in the plays which make up what we now call the theater of the absurd, it is not the former who command the latter, but just the opposite. All of the characters in *The Warrant*, at one time or another, fall victim to the seductive simplicity of the slogans, signs and catch-phrases of mass culture. Pavel is seduced by the signs of power, Varvara — by the signs of chivalry, and Nastya — by the images she appropriates from romance novels. The play develops in the atmosphere of a war among superficially identical, but fundamentally different, vocabularies which obscure meaning, rather than explain, define or clarify experience.

Employing the form of the farce, Erdman pointed toward the danger lurking in such a state of affairs. Pavel may be a mild-mannered simpleton, but when he becomes obsessed with an idea, he immediately takes on the characteristics of a budding tyrant. His demand in the first act that everyone in his household fear him, transforms into symptoms of megalomania in the final act. The point here, of course, is much broader than the mere problem of communism or totalitarianism in Russia. What intrigued Erdman was the false grandeur of the Word. Being a skeptic, he realized that man's deeds seldom match the highfalutin words that describe or justify them.

Erdman effected the shift away from the strictly political or social level by sidestepping the traditional dramatic clash between the old and new worlds. Never in *The Warrant* does there appear a bona fide representative of the new order, the closest thing to it occurring at the end of the play when Ivan Shironkin runs off stage to call the police. But they refuse to appear. All we ever get is the characters' reactions to an undefined, incomprehensible and changing world. As a result, the dramatic conflict unfolds as a tug of war among three rather amorphous states of mind: memories of life in tsarist Russia (which is now extinct), perceptions of life in the Soviet Union (which the characters themselves cannot define and which the spectator never sees) and, finally, the psychological limbo in which all the characters of the play exist. The first scene of *The Warrant*, as Pavel and his mother hang various paintings which will express different attitudes to different potential circumstances, immediately establishes the uncertainty and inner chaos which reigns in the play. It is the internal level which forms the real "setting" of the play, making of it an inquiry into the nature of the unstable relationship between humans and the society which surrounds them, rather than a mere exposé of a particular social order.

Erdman continued to develop his new vision of dramatic structure in *The Suicide*, which comprises a spectacular mixture of the ridiculous and the sublime. Semyon Podsekalnikov is discouraged by his inability to find a job, and a chance comment he makes to his wife Mariya leads her to think he might try to commit suicide. She brings woe upon everyone by appealing for help to Alexander Kalabushkin, an unscrupulous neighbor who is the first to "break the news" to Semyon that he is a potential suicide. After

Semyon's grandiose and pathetically misguided plans to become a profes-
sional tuba player fail resoundingly, Alexander gathers a motley group of
malcontents who encourage the unsuspecting Semyon to dedicate his suicide to various social causes. Aristarkh represents the intelligentsia, Viktor
represents art, Pugachyov represents commerce, and two ladies of ill-
repute, Cleopatra and Raisa, represent spiritual and physical love. But all of
them make essentially identical appeals in which eloquence is reduced to
crass sloganeering. Despite having no desire to commit suicide, the weak-
willed Semyon finds himself being pushed towards it from all sides by these
insistent supplicants. Properly speaking, the play is the study of a man who
is forced to discover for himself reasons to live, rather than reasons to die.

   Semyon's hard-earned discovery comes at a terrible expense, however.
Just as the absence of the outside world in *The Warrant* is symbolized by the
refusal of the police to make an appearance, a crucial role in *The Suicide* is
played by a character who never appears, and about whom we know nothing beyond Viktor's characterization of him as "a marvelous type, a positive
type." This is Fedya Petunin, who "fell in love" with the idea of suicide after
being told of Semyon's supposed plans, and who takes his life off-stage
just as Semyon is finally rejecting the idea for good on-stage. The black
irony of the situation is carried in the play's very title: is this a play about
Semyon or about Fedya Petunin? After all, Petunin is the real suicide.

   The destructive power of mishandled language is everywhere present
in *The Suicide*. Not only does Semyon unexpectedly wind up on the road to
suicide as the result of a simple misunderstanding, but he finds himself
moving inexorably closer to the dreaded act as he is repeatedly seduced by
elegant turns of phrase. In the second act, Aristarkh captures his fancy with
a wonderful vision of a funeral at which Semyon's body will be borne by
"splendid horses in white horsecloths." (Semyon's wide-eyed response is to
exclaim, "Holy Moses! Now that's what I call living!") Later in the same act,
as Semyon hesitates to set a time for his suicide, the group of supplicants
seals the deal by getting him to agree to a farewell banquet. It does not occur
to the dazed Semyon that, by consenting to the banquet, he is consenting to
commit suicide as well. Of course, Fedya Petunin is the play's supreme example of language's potential insidiousness. Obsessed with what he has
been told about Semyon's "suicidal" tendencies, he unwittingly turns lies
into a tragic, irreversible deed.

   The power that words wield, however, can cut two ways. Semyon's sus-
ceptibility to the sublime, which very nearly does him in, is just what saves
him at that very moment when he comes closest of all to taking his life.
While searching in a frenzy for the best place to shoot himself in the fourth
act, he realizes he will never be able to go through with it if he cannot distract himself from what he is doing. In order to bolster his courage, he strikes
up a happy song. But, just as he prepares to pull the trigger, he "hears" the
wailing of a trombone. That wonderful, lively sound is so enticing that he

drops the pistol in total frustration.

This scene, contrasted with the two mentioned above, highlights two of the primary forces at work in *The Suicide*: the lyrical, life-confirming nature of the individual, internal world and the harsh, hostile nature of everything outside it. It is no accident that Semyon is inclined to reject the idea of suicide when he is in isolation, and is drawn closer to it when he is under the influence of others. What little harmony there is in this topsy-turvy world exists only in isolation from social impulses. Semyon's monologues — especially his famous parodical reformulation of Hamlet's speech of "to be or not to be," which he delivers in the eerie presence of a deaf-mute — are masterful examples of the way he works in his own clumsy way towards sublime relevations.

The Suicide is a plea for the autonomy of the individual, although that is not to say it is an apologia for everything the individual stands for or undertakes. Semyon is hardly a traditional, sympathetic character. His abrasive behavior towards his wife and mother-in-law and his tacit complicity in the death of Fedya Petunin both exclude that role for him. At the same time, there is no doubting that he ultimately wins our sympathy. The reason for this can be found by viewing Semyon's predicament in the light of a quote from *Hamlet*, which Erdman lovingly burlesques throughout *The Suicide*. Says Hamlet bitterly, after he has narrowly escaped the deadly designs of Claudius:

> . . . What is a man,
> If his chief good and market of his time
> Be but to sleep and feed? a beast, no more.

But Semyon — who "falls in love with his stomach" as he lies terrified for two days in his coffin, and who can be accused of lacking heroism, character, wisdom, talent and any number of other "positive" traits — is not a beast. He is confused, disenfranchised, and an outcast, but he is no less human for that.

Avoiding anything so formulaic as defenses or accusations — both plays in this volume end on highly paradoxical notes — Erdman sounded the unpopular alarm that heroism cannot be enforced and that the aims of the "crowd" are almost invariably antithetical to the needs of the individual. The themes of *The Warrant* and *The Suicide* — the failure of language as a reliable tool of communication, the degeneration of the human element brought on by the onslaught of mass culture, and the extraordinary, if not always heroic, resilience of the individual human being — remain as contemporary and universal as ever.

JOHN FREEDMAN
Moscow, 1994

A NOTE ON THE TEXTS

There are no canonical texts of either *The Warrant* or *The Suicide*. Neither of the plays was published in Russian during Erdman's lifetime and both underwent numerous rewrites in order to make them suitable either to the censor or to the various theaters which worked on them at one time or another. There exist about a half-dozen "authentic" typescripts of each play. These are copies which were used by Erdman, Meyerhold, Stanislavsky, Erast Garin, Nikolai Okhlopkov and others. If one were to count the samizdat copies which were made over the decades, there are hundreds. All of these variants are similar, but few are identical. For this edition, I have used the most complete of the published texts.

The Warrant is translated from the Russian text edited and published by Wolfgang Kasack in the series Arbeiten und Texte zur Slavistik (No. 10, München: Verlag Otto Sagner in Kommission, 1976). I purposefully disregarded the text published in Nikolai Erdman, *P'esy, intermedii, pis'ma, dokumenty, vospominaniya sovremennikov* (Moscow: Iskusstvo, 1990). It repeats the text published by Lyubov' Rudneva in *Teatr*, No. 10 (1987): 3–28. As indicated by Mikhail Smolyanitsky, this text is a "self-censored" version which the Meyerhold Theater sent to the censorship board in order to get approval for performances.[1]

The Suicide is translated from the most reliable Russian text, published in Nikolai Erdman, *P'esy, intermedii, pis'ma, dokumenty, vospominaniya sovremennikov* (Moscow: Iskusstvo, 1990).

For reference, the other Russian publications of *The Suicide* are: 1) in book form by K-Slavica Publishers, Bremen, Germany, 1973; 2) a serial publication by Lesley Milne in *Novy zhurnal*, No. 112 (1973): 5–24; No. 113 (1973): 5–36; and No. 114 (1974): 5–33; 3) in book form by Ardis Publishers, Ann Arbor, 1980; 4) with an introduction by Alexander Svobodin in *Sovremennaya dramaturgiya*, No. 2 (1987): 186–224. This text, which is repeated in *Teatr pisatelei*, Biblioteka "v pomoshch' khudozhestvennoi samodeyatel'nosti," No. 16 (Moscow: Sovetskaya Rossiya, 1988), is the version that Erdman doctored in the vain hope of making it palatable for publication in the December 1968 issue of *Theater*.

---

[1] Mikhail Smolyanitsky, "Postanovki p'esy N. R. Erdmana 'Mandat' v teatre imeni Vs. Meierkhol'da (epizod iz obshchestvennogo soznaniya serediny 20-kh gg," *Zerkalo istorii* (Moscow: Rossiisky gosudarstvenny gumanitarny universitet, 1992), note 1, 109.

I would like to express my gratitude to Julie A. E. Curtis who combed the translations for rough spots and errors; her numerous suggestions unquestionably made the final versions read more smoothly and accurately. Naturally, she bears no responsibility for those instances where I, perhaps stubbornly, clung to interpretations or renderings that I felt best represented the original.

THE WARRANT

Characters

Nadézhda Petróvna Gulyáchkina
Pável Sergéyevich Gulyáchkin, her son (also called Pavlúsha)
Varvára Sergéyevna Gulyáchkina, her daughter (also called Várya)
Iván Ivánovich Shirónkin, their lodger
Anastasíya Nikoláyevna Púpkina, the Gulyachkin's cook (also called Nástya)
Tamára Leopóldovna Lishnévskaya
Olímp Valeriánovich Smetánich
Valerián Olímpovich Smetánich, his son
Anatóly Olímpovich Smetánich, his youngest son
Avtonóm Sigismúndovich
Agafángel, his servant
Stepán Stepánovich
Felitsiáta Gordéyevna, his wife
Ilínkin
Ilínkina
Zótik Frántsevich Zarkhín
Ariádna Pavlínovna Zarkhiná, his wife
Tósya, their daughter
Syúsya, their daughter
Narkís Smarágdovich Krántik
Father Pavsikákhy
A Janitor
A Hurdy-Gurdy Man
A Drummer
A Woman with a Parrot and Tambourine
A Cabby
Guests

3

ACT I

SCENE ONE

(A room in the Gulyachkin apartment. Pavel stands on a step-ladder hanging paintings. His mother Nadezhda stands beside him. On the floor next to her are framed paintings)

PAVEL. All right now, mother, hand me "Evening in Copenhagen."

NADEZHDA. No, Pavlusha, I think it should be "I Believe in Thee, O Lord."

PAVEL. No, mama, "Evening in Copenhagen" will be more artistic.

NADEZHDA. Well, you know best, Pavlusha. Only I definitely wanted to hang "I Believe in Thee, O Lord" in the middle. It has a prettier frame, Pavlusha. And its content is more profound than "Evening in Copenhagen."

PAVEL. As for the content, mama, take a look at it from another point of view.

NADEZHDA. *(Looking at the other side)* Oh my God! Who is that?

PAVEL. No need to be so frightened, mama. These aren't the old days anymore.

NADEZHDA. Whose mug did you stick on here, Pavlusha?

PAVEL. Read what it says, mama.

NADEZHDA. Hmm. I knew right away he wasn't a Russian. *(Turns the painting around. It is a portrait of Karl Marx)* What's got into you, Pavlusha? These pictures hung side by side for eighteen years. They were pleasing to look at and they never offended a soul.

PAVEL. Mama, you reason like an unconscious element. For example, mama, what, in your opinion, is a picture?

NADEZHDA. How should I know, Pavlusha? I don't read the newspapers.

PAVEL. No, I want you to tell me, mama. In your opinion, what is a picture?

NADEZHDA. In the old days, Pavlusha, there was a post-office clerk who used to take his meals with us. And he always used to say, "Listen here, Nadezhda Petrovna, a picture is nothing but a cry of the soul and a pleasure for the sensory organs."

PAVEL. Maybe that's how it used to be, but these days a picture is nothing but a tool of propaganda.

NADEZHDA. A tool? What do you mean?

PAVEL. It's very simple. Let's say some representative of authority comes to visit us and we have "I Believe in Thee, O Lord" hanging on the wall. A picture like that makes people ask questions. And so he asks, "What did

5

your great-grandfather do, citizeness Gulyachkina?"

NADEZHDA. He didn't do anything. He was the owner of an establishment.

PAVEL. What kind of establishment?

NADEZHDA. A laundry.

PAVEL. A what?

NADEZHDA. A laundry, I said.

PAVEL. A laundry? And what if I arrest you for such bourgeois prejudices?

NADEZHDA. Lord Almighty!

PAVEL. You got that right.

NADEZHDA. How is an honest person supposed to live in the world?

PAVEL. You have to be sneaky, mama. Real sneaky. Don't you pay any mind that I never finished high-school. I see right through this whole revolution.

NADEZHDA. It's a shady business, Pavlusha. You think you can see through it?

PAVEL. Just look through the peep-hole, mama. Look through the peep-hole.

NADEZHDA. The peep-hole? What peep-hole, Pavlusha?

PAVEL. As you know, mama, we have a frosted-glass window in the entryway. So I drilled a hole in it.

NADEZHDA. What did you do that for?

PAVEL. What for? Let's say, for example, somebody rings the doorbell. So you peek through the peep-hole and you see who's come for what. Let's say, for example, it's the chairman of the housing committee, or what's worse, some police commissar.

NADEZHDA. Oh! Lord have mercy on us!

PAVEL. No need for that, mama. As soon as you see some visitor like that through the peep-hole, you immediately turn over the picture and politely usher him into the dining room.

NADEZHDA. And then what?

PAVEL. The commissar will stand there a few minutes and then go away.

NADEZHDA. Why is that, Pavlusha?

PAVEL. Because Karl Marx is the highest boss they've got, mama.

NADEZHDA. You thought it all through wonderfully. Only this man's mug, so to speak, ruins the whole atmosphere of the room.

PAVEL. Don't worry, mama. Whenever we have decent guests, we can turn the picture over and show "Evening in Copenhagen." That way, even if Mister Smetanich himself were to come, he'd say we're not revolutionaries of some sort, but that we're cultured people.

NADEZHDA. In fact, you know what, Pavlusha? Mister Smetanich promised to pay us a visit today.

PAVEL. Why did he do that?

NADEZHDA. No reason. He just said, "I'll come take a look at your son and see how you live."

PAVEL. Why didn't you tell me before, mama? Amazing. Quick, I'll hang up "I Believe in Thee, O Lord." Here, help me move the step-ladder. Is that really what he said, mama? That he wants to take a look at your son?

NADEZHDA. That's what he said.

PAVEL. I don't care what you say, mama, but for an occasion like this I'm putting on a new pair of pants.

NADEZHDA. Wait a minute. I haven't told you yet that Mister Smetanich wants to marry his son to Varya.

PAVEL. Varya?

NADEZHDA. Yes.

PAVEL. His son and Varya?

NADEZHDA. Yes.

PAVEL. Excuse me, mama, but I think your health is failing or perhaps you're sick.

NADEZHDA. No. God is merciful.

PAVEL. But mama, how can he want to marry his son to Varya when he's never even seen our Varya?

NADEZHDA. You think that's bad?

PAVEL. I'm not saying anything, mama. Maybe it would be worse yet if he had seen her. But, somehow, I just can't believe it.

NADEZHDA. You should believe when people tell you things.

PAVEL. Are you telling me, mama, that we're soon going to be relatives of Mister Smetanich?

NADEZHDA. Don't rush things. You should think about the dowry first.

PAVEL. The dowry? Then nothing will come of it, mama. You know yourself that we're bankrupt people.

NADEZHDA. He's not asking for money, Pavlusha.

PAVEL. What does he want then, mama?

NADEZHDA. A fatted calf, my dear.

PAVEL. What do you mean, a fatted calf?

NADEZHDA. The fact is, Pavlusha, he's asking for a communist as Varya's dowry.

PAVEL. A communist?

NADEZHDA. Well, yes.

PAVEL. But mama, how can you offer a live party member as a dowry?

NADEZHDA. Well, you obviously can't just grab one off the street. But if he's one of your own, let's say, a member of the family, I don't see that anyone can forbid that.

PAVEL. Mama, we're good Christians. We don't keep communists here.

NADEZHDA. Don't worry, son. Don't worry, Pavlusha. I'll atone for your sin.

PAVEL. What sin?

NADEZHDA. Well, Pavlusha, you're going to have to join the Party.

7

PAVEL. Me? Join the Party?

NADEZHDA. You, my dear, you. Pavlusha, Mister Smetanich is counting on you.

PAVEL. Mama, hold on to the step-ladder because everything just went black before my eyes.

NADEZHDA. Just think about it, Pavlusha. We'll marry off Varya, I'll go live with Mister Smetanich and before you know it, I'll have educated grandchildren running all around me.

PAVEL. But mama, what am I going to do?

NADEZHDA. What's there to do? People in authority don't do anything. Just ride around in your automobile. Imagine, Pavlusha, you'll start riding around in your automobile and I'll start praying for you. You go for a spin and I'll pray, you go for a spin and I'll pray. Oh, what a life it will be!

PAVEL. Go for a ride? Well all right, mama. I'll think about it. (*Hammers in a nail*)

NADEZHDA. You think about it, Pavlusha! Think about it!

(*Pavel hammers in another nail*)

Oh yes, I also wanted to tell you....

PAVEL. Don't interrupt me, mama. I'm thinking. Ah! I always wanted to be a boss of some kind! As soon as something happened somewhere— wham!—I'd slam the table with my fist. "Silence!" (*Misses the nail head and whacks the wall with his hammer. The sound of falling pots and pans is heard*) There's silence for you.

NADEZHDA. Oh, my Lord! I hope that wasn't our boarder's pots.

SCENE TWO

(*Ivan runs into the room with a shriek. On his head is an overturned pot*)

IVAN. Help! Help! Help, citizens! I'm drowning!

PAVEL. What happened?

IVAN. Ah, so there you are! You'll answer for this, citizen. Rest assured. I'll have justice, citizen.

PAVEL. What right do you have to go around shouting in family surroundings?

IVAN. What do you expect me to do when you try drowning a live man in milk and macaroni?

PAVEL. Excuse me...

IVAN. I certainly will not.

SCENE THREE

(Enter Varvara)

VARVARA. What's the ruckus?

NADEZHDA. What's the problem, Ivan Ivanovich? What happened?

IVAN. Nadezhda Petrovna, how many times have I told you that I am an intellectual laborer? And here you go hammering nails into the wall on purpose.

NADEZHDA. Pardon me, but your nails are no business of ours and our nails are no business of yours. We are in our own room, here.

IVAN. However, Nadezhda Petrovna, I prepare my own meals…

NADEZHDA. Incidentally, the whole house stinks from your meals.

IVAN. I'm sorry, but I'm a bachelor. And unlike some people I know, I don't have any live-in girlfriends to help me. All I have is a paraffin stove. I do have to eat, you know.

NADEZHDA. You might hold your tongue about who lives with you and who doesn't. My daughter is a virgin, you know.

VARVARA. Oh, mother. Don't exaggerate.

IVAN. You expect me to hold my tongue when all I have left over from dinner is some milk and macaroni and you go and knock it over on my head? I'm supposed to keep silent about that, am I?

NADEZHDA. We can't be responsible for your macaroni.

IVAN. Oh, is that right? But you can hammer on the wall as long as it takes for all my pots and pans to fall on my head. What if I had drowned to death in this macaroni? Who would be responsible for that? You or me?

NADEZHDA. If you were a cockroach, Ivan Ivanovich, that would be one thing. But people don't drown in macaroni.

IVAN. The police will tell you whether they do or don't. Rest assured, I won't leave this matter unreported.

NADEZHDA. Ivan Ivanovich, do I look like a criminal or something that you should go around reporting me to the police?

VARVARA. Ivan Ivanovich, you ought to take that pot off your head. It doesn't make a very becoming hat.

IVAN. Oh no you don't. I'm not taking it off. Take it off now and then just try to prove it used to be on your head. No way. I'll tell the commissar, "Look here, comrade commissar, this is hard evidence that the public peace and quiet has been violated." You can call it a pot if you want, but I call it evidence.

NADEZHDA. Are you telling me that you're going to go out on the street with this evidence on your head?

IVAN. I am.

NADEZHDA. They'll put you in an insane asylum.

IVAN. We live in a free society these days. All the insane asylums are closed.

NADEZHDA. Pavlusha, scream something at him please.

PAVEL. How can I scream something at him, mama, when he has such an unpleasant character?

NADEZHDA. Go on, Pavlusha. Don't be afraid, my dear. Otherwise he really will go to the police.

IVAN. Nadezhda Petrovna, I don't advise you to whisper with your son. I am not afraid of your son, Nadezhda Petrovna. I'm not afraid of anybody on earth, Nadezhda Petrovna. I, Nadezhda Petrovna...

PAVEL. Silence! I'm a party man!

(Everyone, beginning with Pavel, is horrified. Ivan begins backing up towards the door and then leaves)

SCENE FOUR

PAVEL. Mama, I'm leaving for the provinces.

VARVARA. What do you mean, you're leaving?

NADEZHDA. What are you leaving for?

PAVEL. Because they can shoot you for saying words like that, mama.

VARVARA and NADEZHDA. Shoot you?

NADEZHDA. Pavlusha, there is no such law that says you can shoot a man for the words he says.

PAVEL. Not all words are equal, mama.

NADEZHDA. I heard all kinds of words when your father was still alive. The late Sergei Tarasych used to say such words that you can't even repeat them in front of an unmarried person. But when he died, it was vodka that killed him, and you tell me...

VARVARA. Mama, don't change the subject. That's not only absurd, it's silly.

PAVEL. But mama, I haven't joined the Party yet.

NADEZHDA. Well then, join.

PAVEL. There's not much I can do about it now. I'll have to.

NADEZHDA. Thank God! Then we can throw a wedding soon. Varvara, thank your brother. He agreed.

VARVARA. *(Extending her hand)* Merci.

PAVEL. But what if they don't take me, mama?

NADEZHDA. Oh, come now, Pavlusha. They take all kinds of derelicts.

PAVEL. In that case, mama, do you know Utkin?

NADEZHDA. You mean the one who crashed his airplane?

PAVEL. That's Utochkin, mama. I'm talking about Utkin.[1]

---

[1] Sergei Utochkin was a pioneer in Russian aviation. Utkin is a humorous name that sounds like Mr. Duck.

NADEZHDA. Then I don't know him.

PAVEL. I met him back when I travelled by train to Samara to buy some bread. To look at him, mama, you'd think he's perfectly normal, but, in fact, he has three relatives who are party members. So here's what I'm going to do, mama. I'm going to invite him over here. Maybe they'll give me a recommendation to get me in the Party.

NADEZHDA. That's a good idea, Pavlusha. Invite them over.

PAVEL. I should also tell you, mama, that if they find out we used to own a grocery store we could wind up in all kinds of trouble.

NADEZHDA. How would they find out about that, Pavlusha? They won't find out.

PAVEL. I just mention it so that you'll be sure to serve them up a hospitable dose of politics.

NADEZHDA. I fixed a sturgeon pie for today, Pavlusha. We can serve them that.

PAVEL. Are you crazy, mama? Do you think communists eat sturgeon? The next thing you'll suggest is crème brûlée or something. We have to show them our Spartan living conditions, and you go suggesting sturgeon pie. And one more thing, mama. In general, if I'm going to be a sacrificial lamb in this family, I demand that everyone here fear me.

NADEZHDA. But, Pavlush…

PAVEL. Silence! For the last time in my life, mama, I demand that, by this evening, all soups in our home be of a proletarian origin. No more "Copenhagens," you got that?

NADEZHDA. Yes, Pavlusha.

PAVEL. And if Varvara says even one more word about God or grocery stores, as God is my witness, I'm heading for the provinces.

VARVARA. This is all rather odd.

PAVEL. That's enough opposition from you, Varvara. One might say that, because of you, a young man at the height of his powers has been reduced to a dowry. You've got no business turning your nose up at him.

NADEZHDA. Varya, ask your brother's forgiveness right now.

VARVARA. But mama…

NADEZHDA. Varvara.

VARVARA. But ma…

NADEZHDA. Varya.

VARVARA. Sorry.

PAVEL. Well, all right then. I'm going now.

NADEZHDA. Where are you going, Pavlusha? To see Utkin?

PAVEL. Yes, mama, to see… Oh my God. I'm done for.

NADEZHDA. What's wrong, Pavlusha?

PAVEL. How can I invite him to visit us when we don't have a single relative from the working class?

11

NADEZHDA. You know I never refuse you anything, Pavlusha, but what we don't have, we don't have.

PAVEL. What if we put over some friends as relatives, mama? Listen, Varya, do you have any friends from the working class?

VARVARA. Maybe I don't even run around with office workers, let alone the working class.

PAVEL. What are we going to do, mama?

NADEZHDA. Wait a minute. Let's ask Nastya. Nastya! Nastya! Oh that little reprobate. She's probably buried in a book again. Nastya!

PAVEL. Varvara, are you deaf or something? Your own mother is screaming her head off and you sit there like a bump on a log.

VARVARA. Shouting is bad for me. My music teacher discovered I'm a coloratura soprano.

PAVEL. Then you can stay a soprano virgin if you want.

NADEZHDA. Do you want to ruin the whole thing? Shout when you're told to shout.

VARVARA. Nastya!

PAVEL. Wow, Varvara! What an incredibly disgusting voice you have.

VARVARA. Disgusting? My music teacher told me…

PAVEL. Your music teacher is an idiot. Nastya!

ALL. Nastya!

VOICE OF NASTYA. Here I am!

ALL. Ah!

SCENE FIVE

(Enter Nastya, the Gulyachkin's cook)

NADEZHDA. What are you shouting about? What are you shouting about, I ask you? Huh? You're in my home, not out on the street somewhere.

NASTYA. I…

NADEZHDA. Shut up when you're being spoken to. You should have been born a foot soldier and not a cook.

NASTYA. I…

NADEZHDA. Don't talk back to me. How come you don't hear us when we're shouting at you? Huh? Are you reading books again? Do you think I pay you so that you can go around buying books all the time?

PAVEL. Mama, settle down. Nastya, I wanted to ask you whether you happen to have any visitors from the working class.

NASTYA. Pavel Sergeyevich! I am a lady.

PAVEL. That's not what I'm talking about. I am asking whether you happen to have acquaintances from the working class.

NASTYA. Unmarried gentlewomen don't have acquaintances.

NADEZHDA. Don't lie to us, Nastya.

NASTYA. Nadezhda Petrovna, I have served many masters and no one has ever observed me with acquaintances. You can run a check if you like.

NADEZHDA. Nastya, I'm telling you, don't lie to us.

NASTYA. Nadezhda Petrovna, if you're talking about Ivan Ivanovich, he's not even a man, he's just a boarder.

NADEZHDA. What?

NASTYA. And even if he did invite me to his room, that was purely for the purposes of enlarging my bust.

PAVEL. For what?

NASTYA. For enlarging my bust.

NADEZHDA. Nastya, you've gone off your rocker. I am preparing to give away my lawful daughter in marriage and, right here in my home, you engage in depravity. Do you think I pay you so that you can go around enlarging your bust? Huh?

VARVARA. Leave her alone, please, mama. This is interesting. Tell me, Nastya, is he really able to enlarge it?

NASTYA. Yes.

VARVARA. How does he do it?

NASTYA. I don't really know how he does it. He suggested it himself. You know, when I lived on Three Saints Lane there was a photography studio located just across the way. It was called "Electric Chic." Naturally, I went over to this "Electric Chic" and ordered half a dozen photos for my own personal enjoyment. But as you know yourself, mademoiselle, the photos they make there are tiny. Your face on them only shows up down to your waist. And since Ivan Ivanovich is a man with what you might call a photographic education, he said to me just yesterday, "Anastasiya Nikolayevna, if you want, I'll enlarge your bust."

VARVARA. You idiot. I got my hopes up for nothing.

NADEZHDA. What kind of nonsense is this? Get out of here right now. Go to the kitchen.

(Nastya leaves)

SCENE SIX

NADEZHDA. Oh, how that girl makes me suffer! Nobody has enough nerves to put up with what I've put up with.

PAVEL. At the present moment, mama, that is a question of secondary importance. You'd be better off telling me what I'm going to do about the relatives I don't have.

VARVARA. You've got a one-track mind. Can't you talk about anything but relatives?

PAVEL. One-track mind? Is that what you said? A one-track mind? I am asking you, did you say I have a one-track mind?

VARVARA. Naturally.

PAVEL. All right Varvara. Here is my ultimatum. Until you find me some relatives from the working class, you can stay a virgin. That's one.

VARVARA. Where am I supposed to find them, Pavel?

PAVEL. I repeat in no uncertain terms, that's one. And your boarder who enlarges busts for other people's cooks, you can just get him out of here. I have no intentions of remaining under one roof with him. That's two.

VARVARA. You really mean get rid of him, Pavel?

PAVEL. Are you saying you won't do it?

VARVARA. Absolutely.

PAVEL. And I say that's two and bye-bye baby. *(Goes out)*

SCENE SEVEN

NADEZHDA. Do as you like, Varvara, but you're going to have to find him some relatives.

VARVARA. He's gotten too big for his britches, mama.

NADEZHDA. Varvara, are you saying that you can't put a little effort into your own happiness? Or do you think that you're the only bride left on earth? Huh?

VARVARA. All right, mama. I'll look for some. That's one. But as for two, how are we going to get rid of him?

NADEZHDA. With noise I think, Varya. With noise.

VARVARA. Noise?

NADEZHDA. Well, yes. You know yourself, Varya, that Ivan Ivanovich can't stand noise. So we'll drive him out with noise.

VARVARA. What noise, mama?

NADEZHDA. That's easy. We can play games of some sort, dance, sing. For instance, if you were to sing him something today, maybe he'd leave right away.

VARVARA. What do you think I am, mama? Chaliapin? I don't even have the voice for that. You'd be better off telling me, mama, is he a brunette?

NADEZHDA. Who? Chaliapin?

VARVARA. No, mama. I mean Mister Smetanich's son.

NADEZHDA. On the contrary. He has brown hair.

VARVARA. Oh, what a shame.

NADEZHDA. How come?

VARVARA. Because blonde women look good when their husbands are brunettes.

NADEZHDA. Are you planning to live with somebody's hair or with a man?

VARVARA. It's a matter of taste, mama. And there's no accounting for taste.

By the way, mama, I literally have no idea what his name is.

NADEZHDA. His name is Valerian, Varya. Valerian Olimpovich Smetanich.

VARVARA. I think Valerian is a wonderful name. Only it sounds a little bit like sleeping pills or something. But basically I'm satisfied.

NADEZHDA. I would hope so. Satisfied isn't the word. Any conscious lady would give her eye tooth to sink her teeth into a man like Valerian Olimpovich. What a soul he has, Varya! What a build he has, Varya! And what a father! Oh, what a father! Just imagine, Varya. This man has been going bankrupt ever since the revolution started, and he still hasn't been able to go bankrupt all the way. It's a wonder the earth can hold a man like that. People of his kind ought to be taken straight to heaven without dying.

VARVARA. What do you think, mama? Should I go to the hairdresser?

NADEZHDA. What for?

VARVARA. To get my hair curled, mama. Plus, I always smell good after I've been to the hairdresser.

NADEZHDA. Good idea, Varya. Go ahead, dear.

VARVARA. Only please don't you tell him anything, mama. Let him think I smell that way on my own. (Leaves)

SCENE EIGHT

NADEZHDA. Lord Almighty! Life? This isn't life. You give away your own daughter in marriage and you're seized by nothing but terror. You live in your own personal home and you have to pay rent for your apartment. Life? This isn't life. And people, look what people have turned into. Young girls aren't only having babies, they're smoking tobacco. And if it's not bad enough that men don't give up their seats to women on trolley cars anymore, they've even stopped doing it for priests. Life? This isn't life. And then look what they've done with the church. In peacetime you could buy a candle for three kopecks and pray as long as your heart desired. And now they say they're going to start taxing every prayerful person for every prayer they utter. At that rate, an all-night service will bankrupt me. They've got another thing coming, though. A true believer can always find a way to pray for free. (During her monologue, Nadezhda spreads out a clean cloth on the table and puts a grammophone on it. She lights candles at either side of the grammophone) It's not for nothing that in the Kireev sons' eighty-sixth Psalm it's written in plain black and white, "Singers and dancers alike say, 'All my springs are in you.'" (She puts on a record and kneels. The music is from a vespers service) Truly is it said, let every breath give praise to God. Lord, Lord, hear his sinner.

SCENE NINE

(Enter Nastya)

NASTYA. Madame.
NADEZHDA. Ah! You idiot. You're always sneaking up on me during my prayers.
NASTYA. Madame, some lady is asking for you.
NADEZHDA. What lady?
NASTYA. I've never seen her. However, here she is herself.

SCENE TEN

(Enter Tamara)

NADEZHDA. Is that you, Tamara Leopoldovna? Come in, come in, please. Lord Almighty, what a pleasant surprise. Nastya, stop the service.
TAMARA. Bring it in. Bring it right in here.

SCENE ELEVEN

(Two men carry in a trunk)

NADEZHDA. Heavens! Are you moving in with me Tamara Leopoldovna?
TAMARA. Oh, don't ask, Nadezhda Petrovna.
NADEZHDA. Oh, I don't understand, Tamara Leopoldovna.
TAMARA. Oh, it's simply awful, Nadezhda Petrovna.
NADEZHDA. Oh, you're frightening me, Tamara Leopoldovna.
TAMARA. Oh, don't speak about it, Nadezhda Petrovna. Put it right here. That's it. I won't be needing you any more.
NADEZHDA. Nastya, show these men the door.

(Nastya and the two men leave)

SCENE TWELVE

NADEZHDA. Sit down, sit down, Tamara Leopoldovna. Not there, not there, Tamara Leopoldovna. Right here in the easy chair with the little pillow.
TAMARA. Oh, it makes no difference.
NADEZHDA. How is your health, Tamara Leopoldovna? Are you feeling well?
TAMARA. Can't you see for yourself that I'm not myself at all?

NADEZHDA. Heavens! Don't tell me you've had some misfortune.

TAMARA. Oh, what a nightmare. Oh, what a nightmare. Just imagine, Nadezhda Petrovna, we are expecting a search this evening.

NADEZHDA. A search? In the Lord's name, may they all be damned. How can it possibly be, Tamara Leopoldovna, that someone would up and want to search such a fine woman as you, Tamara Leopoldovna?

TAMARA. You don't really think that men are capable of appreciating a fine woman, do you, Nadezhda Petrovna?

NADEZHDA. What are these accursed people planning to search you for?

TAMARA. You're so naive, Nadezhda Petrovna. It's obvious for what. Does anybody need a reason to do anything any more? I could understand it, Nadezhda Petrovna, if my husband were serving in the organs. I don't deny it, it's true that in the course of service one can occasionally..., oh, what do you call it? One can occasionally spring a leak, or something. You know, a slip of the pen or the tongue, or something like that. But I repeat, Nadezhda Petrovna, my husband doesn't serve anywhere at all. And now it turns out that you can't live and not serve the organs. But, tell me this, if he has to serve, that means he has to work. And if he has to work, then how will he ever be able to earn a living?

NADEZHDA. Oh, life. This isn't life.

TAMARA. You're telling me. Such a great country, and—boom!—a revolution. One is simply ashamed before the other monarchies. Can such a dim-witted people really understand an idea? You know, Nadezhda Petrovna, my husband always said, "If they'd have a revolution a hundred years from now, I'd definitely support it."

NADEZHDA. What are you going to do now, Tamara Leopoldovna?

TAMARA. I have a favor to ask of you, Nadezhda Petrovna. Only I don't know whether you'll agree to it.

NADEZHDA. But of course, Tamara Leopoldovna. For you, Tamara Leopoldovna, I'd.... Why, you were once our best customer, Tamara Leopoldovna.

TAMARA. In that case, take this trunk off my hands.

NADEZHDA. That's all?

TAMARA. Oh my, no. This trunk is very dangerous.

NADEZHDA. Dangerous?

TAMARA. Look here. (*Opens the trunk*)

NADEZHDA. A dress? I thought there was a bomb inside.

TAMARA. Oh, if only you knew whose dress this was, Nadezhda Petrovna.

NADEZHDA. You mean it's not yours, Tamara Leopoldovna?

TAMARA. Oh, don't even ask, Nadezhda Petrovna.

NADEZHDA. Oh, then whose is it, Tamara Leopoldovna?

TAMARA. Oh, don't even speak about it, Nadezhda Petrovna.

NADEZHDA. Oh, you can tell me, Tamara Leopoldovna.

17

TAMARA. Well then listen, Nadezhda Petrovna. This dress.... Close the door, Nadezhda Petrovna.

NADEZHDA. There, it's closed, Tamara Leopoldovna.

TAMARA. This dress... belonged to Alexandra Fyodorovna.

NADEZHDA. What Alexandra Fyodorovna? You mean the midwife Alexandra Fyodorovna who gave birth to my Pavlusha with me?

TAMARA. What midwife, Nadezhda Petrovna? I'm talking about the empress.

NADEZHDA. The emp.... Oh, Tamara Leopoldovna!

TAMARA. "Oh" is right, Nadezhda Petrovna.

NADEZHDA. How did it fall into your hands, Tamara Leopoldovna?

TAMARA. Oh, it's a long story. Can you imagine it? In the old days my husband had an aunt. This aunt had a son who lived in Petersburg. And can you imagine it, a genuine lady-in-waiting was the godmother of the eldest daughter of the landlady of my husband's aunt's very own son. So when the terrible catastrophe took place, everyone began scrambling to save Russia. And her Excellency's lady-in-waiting, the godmother of the eldest daughter of the landlady of my husband's aunt's son, saved this dress. But since Russia didn't stop its hell-bent slide into ruin, the landlady of my husband's aunt's son, in her turn, was forced to save the dress for the lady-in-waiting. Then my husband's aunt's son saved the dress for the landlady, my husband's aunt saved it for her son, and finally, my husband saved it for his aunt. In short, if they find out that we saved this dress, we're doomed.

NADEZHDA. What a horrible story. You'd better get rid of it, Tamara Leopoldovna.

TAMARA. You're crazy, Nadezhda Petrovna. Don't you realize, Nadezhda Petrovna, that this trunk contains everything that is left of Russia in Russia? And who can we count on to save Russia these days if not ourselves, Nadezhda Petrovna?

NADEZHDA. That's true, Tamara Leopoldovna.

TAMARA. And then, Nadezhda Petrovna, if the French are able to slip some sort of tsar into Russia in the near future, perhaps they'll give my husband a medal for saving this dress.

NADEZHDA. A medal? What sort of medal?

TAMARA. What sort? I don't know. Maybe an order of some kind or a small pension.

NADEZHDA. A pension? In that case, Tamara Leopoldovna, please don't forget to petition on our account.

TAMARA. How can you even ask, Nadezhda Petrovna? For heroism like this, we'll be happy to petition for you.

NADEZHDA. Oh, I'm just doing this for you, Tamara Leopoldovna.

TAMARA. Not for me, Nadezhda Petrovna. For Russia.

NADEZHDA. Oh, when-oh-when will the old days return?

TAMARA. Just this morning, my husband said to me, "Tamara sweetheart, peek through the window, please, and tell me, has the Soviet state collapsed yet?" "No," I said to him, "It seems to be holding strong." "Oh well, Tamara dear," he said, "draw the curtains and we'll look again tomorrow."

NADEZHDA. But when will tomorrow come?

TAMARA. Patience, Nadezhda Petrovna, patience. And in the meantime, take this. *(Pulls out a pistol)*

NADEZHDA. Heavens! A pistol!

TAMARA. Don't be afraid, Nadezhda Petrovna.

NADEZHDA. But what if it shoots?

TAMARA. If you don't touch it, Nadezhda Petrovna, it won't shoot. Even so, I'll feel safer for the dress's sake. And so guard it well and have faith in God.

NADEZHDA. I do have faith, Tamara Leopoldovna, I do have faith. But I don't know who you can have faith in anymore when, other than God, there are no good people left in Moscow.

TAMARA. Well, farewell, Nadezhda Petrovna. And remember, mum's the word.

NADEZHDA. I'll be as silent as the grave, Tamara Leopoldovna. God be with you.

(Tamara leaves)

SCENE THIRTEEN

NADEZHDA. Lord Almighty! Lord Almighty! Life? This isn't life. Well, I'll just finish praying now and then I'll look to see if the sturgeon pie is ready. Lord! O Lord! You are my last redeemer. *(Puts a record on the grammophone)* Hear my prayer, my kind and loving Lord. *(The record plays a raucous can-can)* Damn! I put the wrong record on!

END OF ACT I

ACT II

SCENE ONE

(Nastya is reading a book)

NASTYA. *(Reading)* "'Milord,' cried the princess, 'I never said I loved you. You are mistaken.' 'Princess,' cried milord, 'take my sabre and run me through.'" Oh, what a desperate character this milord is! How charming. "'You poor, unfortunate man,' cried the princess, 'then you truly do love me?' 'Alas,' cried milord, 'do I love you? I love you as a bird loves freedom.'" Oh what a charming man this milord is! It's simply amazing. "'In that case,' cried the princess, 'I cast off my mask of deception.' And they joined their lips in ecstasy." Lord Almighty, what a life! And that's the kind of life they destroyed. If only our government had known what a princess's life was like, it could never have done what it did. "But love is as a mirage, and into the room marched the duke." Uh-oh. Now there's going to be fireworks. This duke is a terribly typical man. No matter who he meets, he gives them an earful.

SCENE TWO

(Enter Ivan)

NASTYA. "'Scoundrel,' cried the duke. 'You have no right being in this room.'"
IVAN. How can you talk to me like that, Anastasiya Nikolayevna?
NASTYA. "'Scoundrel! Behind my back you deprive me of my honor!'"
IVAN. As God is my witness, Anastasiya Nikolayevna, it's not true. I give you my word, that's just the way it seemed.
NASTYA. Oh! Ivan Ivanovich.
IVAN. Believe me, Anastasiya Nikolayevna, a woman's honor for me is not just an empty word. It's my whole reason for being. However, Anastasiya Nikolayevna, I do sense the moral need to find solace in a woman's soul.
NASTYA. What are you saying, Ivan Ivanovich?
IVAN. Remember, Anastasiya Nikolayevna, I am a bachelor and I have no one to patch my linen. Furthermore, you are a hefty woman and a man could easily lose himself in you.
NASTYA. Ivan Ivanovich, I am a rather young lady and I am forbidden to

understand whatever it is you're talking about.

IVAN. And please, Anastasiya Nikolayevna, don't give a thought to my moustache. At heart, Anastasiya Nikolayevna, I am truly a child.

NASTYA. No, no! What makes you say so? A moustache is a gift from God. Only you shouldn't wear it inside out, Ivan Ivanovich.

IVAN. What do you mean, inside out?

NASTYA. You let it dangle downwards, Ivan Ivanovich. You should make it stand up in the air. Then it will be a sight for anyone's sore eyes.

IVAN. Anastasiya Nikolayevna, a man's moustache requires a woman's caresses. Otherwise, it can't possibly grow as it should. But should your hands give it the proper prompting, it will remain in everlasting bliss.

NASTYA. Oh, Ivan Ivanovich. I couldn't.

IVAN. You can, Anastasiya Nikolayevna. Believe me, you can.

NASTYA. Oh, no.

IVAN. Just give it a little try.

NASTYA. But why should I go touching somebody else's moustache?

IVAN. For curiosity's sake if nothing else, Anastasiya Nikolayevna.

NASTYA. Well, if only for curiosity's sake, Ivan Ivanovich. But don't go getting any ideas in your head.

IVAN. Anastasiya Nikolayevna, I never have any thoughts in my head.

NASTYA. In that case, I'll try. Hmm, No matter what I do it won't stand up. You probably had a moustache like that from birth.

IVAN. Wet your fingers a bit, Anastasiya Nikolayevna.

NASTYA. Oh, with pleasure.

IVAN. Believe me, Anastasiya Nikolayevna, you are penetrating through my moustache to my very heart.

NASTYA. Milord, I never said I loved you. You are forgetting yourself.

IVAN. Pardon me. That was just an impulse of madness. However, Anastasiya Nikolayevna, you should know that when it comes to love, I fear nothing. If you would like to join with me for eternity, I am willing.

NASTYA. Your personality is but little known to me. I can't possibly know whether you may even have children somewhere.

IVAN. Anastasiya Nikolayevna, children are no shame. They are a misfortune. But if you have reservations about my exterior appearance....

NASTYA. Oh, no. Your exterior appearance is quite proportional.

IVAN. Or, perhaps, concerning the manner in which I dress?

NASTYA. Oh, no. Nothing like that.

IVAN. Because, if you take a close look at my necktie, you will notice that I dress with great comfort.

NASTYA. You have a very handsome necktie. Only why have you tied it up with macaroni?

IVAN. What macaroni?

NASTYA. Right here, Ivan Ivanovich. A string of genuine macaroni.

IVAN. Oh, that scoundrel.

NASTYA. Cried the duke.

IVAN. What?

NASTYA. Just a reflex. But tell me, who are you talking about, if you'll pardon my expression.

IVAN. Who else? Pavel Sergeyevich, of course.

NASTYA. Pavel Sergeyevich?

IVAN. Incidentally, tell me please, when did your Pavel Sergeyevich find time to join the Party?

NASTYA. He hasn't joined any parties, Ivan Ivanovich.

IVAN. How's that?

NASTYA. Quite simple.

IVAN. He didn't join the Party? Quick! Where did you put that strand of macaroni you took off my tie?

NASTYA. On the floor, Ivan Ivanovich.

IVAN. On the floor? Where is it?

NASTYA. You're wasting your time looking for it, Ivan Ivanovich. Because eating macaroni that you've already stepped on is very dangerous for the stomach.

IVAN. Just give it to me quick, please. I'll be right back. *(Leaves)*

SCENE THREE

NASTYA. Oh, how he expressed his feelings so delicately and then, all of a sudden, macaroni. Ah, here it is, I think. Yes, that's it. Just imagine, such a tiny piece of dough and it's capable of destroying dreams. If he was just making fun of me with everything he said, then he should be rather ashamed. But if he wasn't just making fun of me, then I'm prepared to throw off my mask of deception and tell him, "I'm willing." Joining for eternity with a gentleman like Ivan Ivanovich would be pleasant entertainment for any girl.

SCENE FOUR

(Enter Ivan)

IVAN. Well? Did you find it?

NASTYA. Lord Almighty, Ivan Ivanovich, why did you put a pot on your head?

IVAN. For God's sake, don't say that I put it on. Let them think that I never took it off.

NASTYA. What do you mean, you never took it off? Are you telling me that you ordinarily go around in a pot, Ivan Ivanovich?

IVAN. I am temporarily compelled to. But where is my macaroni, Anastasiya Nikolayevna?

NASTYA. First of all, Ivan Ivanovich, you ought to wipe the dirt off with a rag.

IVAN. On the contrary, Anastasiya Nikolayevna. The dirtier the better. Let impartial justice see how former landlords bury hard-working citizens in filth by means of milk and macaroni.

NASTYA. Ivan Ivanovich, where are you going, looking like that?

IVAN. To the police, Anastasiya Nikolayevna. To the police. (Leaves)

SCENE FIVE

NASTYA. To the police? Ivan Ivanovich! Ivan Ivanovich! Come back! For heaven's sake, come back, I tell you! He's gone. Obviously, once the police get hold of a man in head attire like that, they'll never let him back out again. Oh no! Sounds like someone is trying to sneak in the back door. It's probably the mistress. I'd better hide "The Martyr Queen" under my pillow. Nadezhda Petrovna is opposed to all forms of self-education. (Leaves)

SCENE SIX

(Enter Varvara)

VARVARA. Come in. Come in.

SCENE SEVEN

(Enter the Hurdy-Gurdy Man)

VARVARA. Stand up against this wall and begin, please. Well? What are you waiting for?

HURDY-GURDY MAN. It's all the same to me, of course, but I think I'd better go out on the street and you can listen to me through the window.

VARVARA. What?

HURDY-GURDY MAN. I don't like wasting words, miss, but my music is outdoors music.

VARVARA. Why, you're nothing but a cheat. How come you agreed earlier to do what I asked you?

HURDY-GURDY MAN. I thought you were inviting me to a birthday party or a drunken orgy of some sort. I don't play in private living quarters for an audience of one.

VARVARA. But don't you understand? The point is to drive someone out.

HURDY-GURDY MAN. I understand perfectly. Lots of people are being driven out of their minds these days because old heads can't fathom the new life.

VARVARA. We're not driving anyone out of their mind, we're driving a boarder out of our apartment.

HURDY-GURDY MAN. Oh, a boarder. Oh, well that's a different story. What are you driving him out for, mademoiselle?

VARVARA. Because he's a hooligan. Can you imagine? He wants to make me a virgin to the end of my days.

HURDY-GURDY MAN. Oh, come now, mademoiselle. How could he possibly make a virgin out of you?

VARVARA. You probably have not noticed that I am a bride. That's right, a bride. Well, this morning my brother Pavel Sergeyevich posed an ultimatum concerning this boarder of ours. He said, "If you don't drive him out of our apartment, then you can just stay a virgin."

HURDY-GURDY MAN. Yes, well of course that's a shame. Because virginity is a little bit like a guard dog. He may not partake himself, but he doesn't let anyone else get at the goods either.

VARVARA. Exactly. So mama and I have decided to drive him out.

HURDY-GURDY MAN. I see. What kind of music do you adore most?

VARVARA. Hymns.

HURDY-GURDY MAN. Mademoiselle, I have a Soviet instrument. It doesn't play church music.

VARVARA. Well then, play what ever you can, only play it loud.

(The Hurdy-Gurdy Man plays, Varvara sings)

VOICE OF NASTYA. I'm coming, Varvara Sergeyevna! Don't panic! I'll be right there!

SCENE EIGHT

(Nastya enters at a run)

NASTYA. Here I am. Holy Mother of God! She's alive! She's alive!

VARVARA. Who's alive?

NASTYA. You, Varvara Sergeyevna. You're alive, thank God. You're alive.

VARVARA. Have you gone insane? Or have you just gone out of your mind?

NASTYA. What do you mean, Varvara Sergeyevna? I was just standing in the kitchen with the neighbor's cook and she says to me, "I think somebody's murdering your Varvara Sergeyevna, because she's screaming in an unearthly voice."

VARVARA. Who has an unearthly voice? First of all, that's what my own personal voice sounds like and, second of all, you're an idiot.

NASTYA. These are dangerous times, Varvara Sergeyevna. How was I to know?

VARVARA. That's enough talk from you. Start dancing!

NASTYA. What?

VARVARA. Start dancing, I told you.

NASTYA. I don't dance, mademoiselle.

VARVARA. What do you mean, you don't dance? If we hired you to do any dirty work we want, you don't have the full right to refuse our demands. And if I tell you to dance, that means you dance. Play on, play on, dear man. Sing. Sing louder. Nastya, dance. Dance louder. Like they do at royal ceremonies. What am I doing? Wait! Wait a minute! Nastya, come here. Smell me. Have I lost my smell? Well? Speak up. Have I? Do I still smell?

NASTYA. You smell a little bit.

VARVARA. Thank God. Otherwise, all this dancing could make all my aroma from the hairdressers fly right out the window. I'm trying to preserve my aroma for Valerian Olimpovich.

HURDY-GURDY MAN. I have a feeling that he's already packing, mademoiselle. Because I've already broken a sweat.

NASTYA. Who is packing?

VARVARA. Ivan Ivanovich.

NASTYA. Ivan Ivanovich? He's not here.

VARVARA. Where is he?

NASTYA. Who?

VARVARA. Ivan Ivanovich.

NASTYA. Ivan Ivanovich?

VARVARA. Yes.

NASTYA. In a pot.

VARVARA. Where?

NASTYA. That is, I meant to say that he is probably..., that he has probably gone.

VARVARA. You mean we've been playing for nothing?

HURDY-GURDY MAN. No.

VARVARA. What do you mean, no?

HURDY-GURDY MAN. I mean, no. Maybe you were singing for nothing, but you will be kind to pay me what I am owed for my music.

VARVARA. Wait a minute. Who are you?

HURDY-GURDY MAN. What do you mean, who?

VARVARA. I mean, who are you?

HURDY-GURDY MAN. Me? I'm a folk artist.

VARVARA. No, I mean what's your class?

HURDY-GURDY MAN. Oh, my class? I finished two years at the religious seminary.

VARVARA. That's not what I'm talking about. Are you from the working class?

HURDY-GURDY MAN. No. My background is artificial. I'm a self-taught artist.

VARVARA. Oh, what a shame.

HURDY-GURDY MAN. What's it to you?

VARVARA. It's nothing to me. It's my brother I was thinking about. You see, I promised him I'd find some relatives from the working class.

HURDY-GURDY MAN. Relatives?

VARVARA. Exactly. You see, some members of the Bolshevik Party are supposed to pay him a visit today, but he doesn't have any relatives from the working class.

HURDY-GURDY MAN. Why didn't you do something about that before…, uh…, mademoiselle?

VARVARA. Because before, you didn't need relatives to do your work for you.

HURDY-GURDY MAN. So what are you planning to do, mademoiselle?

VARVARA. I've got to rent some proletarians. Only, where will I ever find them?

HURDY-GURDY MAN. Ah, finding rapscallions like that is easy.

VARVARA. Listen. Maybe you could help me.

HURDY-GURDY MAN. What makes you think I can't?

VARVARA. You see, mama baked a sturgeon pie today and then we'll also have a whole lot of French candy. Basically, we're prepared to go to any lengths for the working class.

HURDY-GURDY MAN. That's for the body. What are you prepared to offer for the soul?

VARVARA. What do you mean, for the soul?

HURDY-GURDY MAN. Well, for example, will you have spirits?

VARVARA. We will.

HURDY-GURDY MAN. You will?

VARVARA. We will.

HURDY-GURDY MAN. I can't for the life of me figure out how it slipped my mind.

VARVARA. What's that?

HURDY-GURDY MAN. You see, it just so happens that I'm from the working class myself.

VARVARA. Oh, what a surprise!

HURDY-GURDY MAN. Tell me, mademoiselle, what quantity of relatives will you be needing?

VARVARA. I would say three people will do. One relative for every communist.

HURDY-GURDY MAN. Well, I would say there ought to be one bottle for every relative.

VARVARA. In that case, we'll be expecting you.

HURDY-GURDY MAN. It's a deal.

VARVARA. Nastya. See this gentleman out the servants entrance and pick up three bottles of port at the grocery store. Got that?

NASTYA. Got it, mademoiselle.

VARVARA. Step to it!

(Nastya and the Hurdy-Gurdy Man leave)

SCENE NINE

VARVARA. Cares, cares. Nothing but cares and no fun. Once a month you get to go to the hairdresser and that's the only fun you have. Mama doesn't let me go to church anymore. She's says I might get killed. The bathhouse is filled with all kinds of riffraff these days. It's no fun going there. Basically, in the arisen situation there's simply nowhere for a cultured girl to go. But all I want to know is whether Valerian Olimpovich will like me or not. I think he'll like me. I have a very beautiful soul and eyelashes. Plus, my smile is very becoming to my face. Only, it's too bad that it doesn't fit on this mirror.

SCENE TEN

(Enter Pavel)

PAVEL. Varya, what are you making ugly faces for?

VARVARA. I think they quite suit me.

PAVEL. With a mug like yours, any ugly face would suit you. Only, you'd better think about your brother too, Varvara. For instance, does a sister like you suit him?

VARVARA. Pavlusha, that's not my mug, it's my smile.

PAVEL. Your smile, huh? Being an honest person, I declare here and now that if you greet my guests this evening with smiles like that I'll renounce you.

VARVARA. You can't renounce me.

PAVEL. And I'm telling you that I'll not only renounce you, I'll disgrace you for life.

VARVARA. How could you possibly disgrace me?

PAVEL. Simple. I'll say you're my aunt, not my sister.

VARVARA. Pavel, how can you call me such names when I went out and

27

found you a relative? What impudence.

PAVEL. You did? Is he a worker?

VARVARA. He is.

PAVEL. What kind of work does he do?

VARVARA. He works with his hands. So, are your communists coming?

PAVEL. They are. Utkin himself promised to bring them.

VARVARA. Then you might say you're almost a full-fledged party member now.

PAVEL. From head to toe. Look, I even bought a briefcase. Only I don't have a party i.d. card yet.

VARVARA. So what, Pavel? If you have a briefcase, any door will open for you even without a party i.d. card.

PAVEL. Varya! A new life is beginning! Oh, by the way, do you happen to know what the R.C.P. is, Varya?[1]

VARVARA. The R.C.P? No. Why do you need to know?

PAVEL. Because Utkin told me, "These days, every idiot knows what the R.C.P. is."

VARVARA. In that case, how come you don't know, Pavlusha?

PAVEL. Well, I probably used to know. But a party man has so much to think about, sometime he goes and forgets.

VARVARA. Pavel, look. A trunk.

PAVEL. A trunk? Where?

VARVARA. Right here.

PAVEL. I'll be darned. A trunk.

VARVARA. Strange.

PAVEL. I'd say it's darned strange.

VARVARA. What could be in it?

PAVEL. Take a look.

VARVARA. There's a lock on it, Pavel.

PAVEL. I'll be darned. A lock.

VARVARA. Amazing.

PAVEL. I'd say it's darned amazing. How come mama is always complaining that we have nothing left in our trunks? If you ask her, "Mama, where are papa's trousers," she always says, "We ate them up, Pavlusha, we ate them up. Back in nineteen-eighteen we traded all of our belongings for flour and we ate it all up." And then, Varya, if you ask her for money, she always says, "How could we possibly have any money, Pavlusha? They took it all away from us in nineteen-eighteen." So then you ask her, "What do we live on, mama?" And she says, "Pavlusha, we're eating up the last of your father's trousers." Can you imagine what papa's trousers must have been like if they're enough to sustain an entire family?

---

[1] The Russian Communist Party.

VARVARA. Well, it looks like mama still has something left over beside papa's trousers.

PAVEL. It looks like it, Varya. Otherwise, why would she lock up her trunks?

VARVARA. Pavel, it's just a tiny little lock.

PAVEL. Yeah. It's not much of a lock.

VARVARA. I'll bet you could open a lock like that with a fork.

PAVEL. A fork? I don't think a fork would do it. But a nail would definitely do the trick.

VARVARA. Wait a second. *(Gives him a nail)*

PAVEL. What if we get caught?

VARVARA. Who'd catch us, Pavel? By all appearances, we're honest people. Nobody would ever suspect us.

PAVEL. What if mama found out?

VARVARA. Mama would instantly suspect Nastya, because all cooks are crooks. And our cook is probably a crook too.

PAVEL. Yeah. I'll bet she's definitely a crook, Varvara. She's got something awful strange about her eyes.

VARVARA. She's a crook, Pavel. A crook.

PAVEL. It's simply unbelievable how many dishonest people there are these days.

VARVARA. Pavel, do you need some light? *(Takes the lamp off the table)*

PAVEL. That's it. Shine it right here. Put it on the floor.

(Varvara puts the lamp on the floor)

SCENE ELEVEN

(Enter Nadezhda)

NADEZHDA. There seems to be some sort of an eclipse in here. Mother Redeemer, what if someone is trying to break into the imperial dress?

VARVARA. Well, is it giving yet?

PAVEL. It's giving. Any minute now.

NADEZHDA. Thieves! Somebody is breaking in. Where did I put that pistol? Oh, Lord. Oh, Lord Almighty, here it is. The desperadoes will see me. As God is my witness, they'll see me. Oh, no! They're getting up. Help! I'll shoot!

VARVARA. Help! Thieves!

PAVEL. Get down! They'll shoot!

NADEZHDA. Help!

PAVEL and VARVARA. Help!

NADEZHDA. They're probably bolsheviks or bandits of some sort.

PAVEL. Comrade!

NADEZHDA. That settles that. Bolsheviks. I only pray they don't shoot. Please, don't let them shoot! *(The pistol fires)*

PAVEL. Varya, touch me. Am I alive?

VARVARA. I think so.

NADEZHDA. Lordy heavens! I've given myself a concussion.

PAVEL. What about you?

VARVARA. I think I'm only barely alive.

NADEZHDA. They're whispering. I can hear them whispering. They've probably come to arrest me, the desperadoes. Oh, they're going to arrest me.

PAVEL. Comrade! Please note that we are children. Word of honor, we're only children. The hope of the future, as they say.

NADEZHDA. It was Tamara Leopoldovna who dumped that dress on me. Word of honor, it was Tamara Leopoldovna.

PAVEL. Comrade, what good will it do you to shoot us? When our mama comes in a minute, shoot her.

NADEZHDA. Tell me straight out, are you bolsheviks or bandits?

PAVEL. We're unaligned, comrade. Third-rate unaligned.

NADEZHDA. Glory be to God! They're only bandits. Help! Thieves!

VARVARA. Help! Murder!

PAVEL. Comrade! Mama!

NADEZHDA. Help! I'll shoot!

PAVEL. Mama, what are you doing? It's me, Pavel!

NADEZHDA. You? Is it really you?

PAVEL. It's me, mama. It's me.

VARVARA. It's him, mama. It's him.

PAVEL. What's wrong with you, mama? Can't you see for yourself?

NADEZHDA. How do you think I can see, Pavel, when I've got both eyes shut tight?

PAVEL. Mama! Open your eyes this instant. Otherwise there may be a catastrophe.

NADEZHDA. How can I open them, Pavlusha, when this pistol is going to go off at any second?

PAVEL. She's going to shoot! Varya, hit the deck! Mama! You're aiming at me again! Turn it around, mama. Turn it on yourself. The barrel, the barrel. Turn the barrel on yourself. Aim at yourself. Aim at yourself, I tell you. For God's sake, otherwise you're going to shoot us!

NADEZHDA. It's going to explode, Pavlusha. As God is my witness, it's going to explode!

PAVEL. Duck, Varya!

VARVARA. Mama, put it down somewhere!

NADEZHDA. Varya, how can I put it down when the slightest movement will make it fire?

PAVEL. Mama, what got into your head to turn our apartment into a civil war zone?

VARVARA. Mama, I have a feeling it's beginning to shoot.

NADEZHDA. Children mine! Pay my respects to Mister Smetanich. I'm dying. It's going to explode. (Drops the pistol on the chair)

PAVEL. Did it miss me?

VARVARA. Where did it fall, mama?

NADEZHDA. On the chair.

PAVEL. Now explain, please, mama. Where did you get a firearm?

NADEZHDA. Tamara Leopoldovna gave it to me, Pavlusha.

PAVEL. What for?

NADEZHDA. For the dress's self-defense, Pavlusha.

VARVARA. The dress?

PAVEL. What dress?

NADEZHDA. The dress that used to contain our whole empire, Pavlusha.

VARVARA. And what contains it now, mama?

NADEZHDA. The trunk, Varya.

PAVEL. How does it fit in there, mama?

NADEZHDA. Because, Pavlusha, they shook the whole empire right out of it.

VARVARA. Whose dress is it, mama?

NADEZHDA. First of all, swear to God that you won't tell a soul, because I already swore to God that I wouldn't tell.

VARVARA. I swear to God, I won't tell.

PAVEL. I can't swear to God. These days we're ruled by a dictatorship of the proletariat.

VARVARA. Go ahead and swear, Pavel. The proletariat will never hear.

PAVEL. I swear to God, I won't tell.

NADEZHDA. This dress, my children, belonged to our sovereign, the Empress Alexandra Fyodorovna.

VARVARA. Oh, how interesting.

PAVEL. Pardon my hinting, mama, but that's a lie.

NADEZHDA. I'm not lying any more than I do at confession. Look for yourself, if you want.

PAVEL. Mama! It's almost brand new.

VARVARA. Only the armpits are a bit worn.

NADEZHDA. That's from regal sweat, Varya.

VARVARA. Because she worked so hard?

PAVEL. What are you talking about, Varya? Do you think the empress ever did any work?

VARVARA. Then what did she sweat for, mama?

NADEZHDA. From praying.

VARVARA. Oh, that must have been an awfully bold seamstress not to fear sewing dresses for the sovereign.

PAVEL. You idiot, Varya. Seamstresses don't sew for sovereigns.

VARVARA. Then who does?

PAVEL. A general's wife of some kind. Or maybe even a countess.

VARVARA. Mama, I wish we could see what it looks like when there's a woman in it.

PAVEL. There aren't any women like that in Russia anymore.

VARVARA. What if I tried it on?

NADEZHDA. You?

PAVEL. You don't have enough of a build to wear a dress like that.

VARVARA. I always was offended at you for making me so short, mama.

SCENE TWELVE

(Enter Nastya)

NASTYA. Here are your three bottles, mademoiselle.

PAVEL. Nastya, snap to attention and don't move!

NASTYA. What?

PAVEL. Snap to attention, I say. Look, mama, Nastya is just the right size.

NADEZHDA. But what's the point, Pavlusha?

PAVEL. For the illusion of a regal life, mama.

NADEZHDA. Well, of course, I'd be curious to see myself. Only, what if someone finds out?

VARVARA. We'll just put it on for a second and then stash it away again.

NADEZHDA. I don't think we should, Varya. She's a dirty woman. After all, she works in the kitchen.

VARVARA. Yes, she is dirty. Nastya, go get my perfume soap in the washroom and I'll scrub your ears myself.

NASTYA. What for, mademoiselle?

VARVARA. For…, how did you put it, Pavlusha?

PAVEL. For the illusion of a regal life.

VARVARA. That's it exactly. Let's go.

(Varvara, carrying the dress, leaves with Nastya)

SCENE THIRTEEN

NADEZHDA. You know what, Pavlusha? Tamara Leopoldovna promised to petition for a pension for me.

PAVEL. A pension for what?

NADEZHDA. For saving Russia.

PAVEL. What do you mean, for saving Russia? First of all, the communists will never let you to save Russia.

NADEZHDA. Pavlusha, who cares what they want when any day now the French are going to sneak a tsar into Russia?

PAVEL. What tsar? Do you realize what you are saying, mama? If somebody really does sneak a tsar into Russia, the first thing they'll do is hang me, no questions asked. After that, you just try to prove that I'm only a dowry and not a communist.

NADEZHDA. That's where the dress will save you.

PAVEL. Mama, I oppose this dress with every fibre in my body.

NADEZHDA. But, Pavel.

PAVEL. If we don't liquidate it this instant, then somebody else is going to liquidate me.

NADEZHDA. But what about the pension, Pavel?

PAVEL. Mama, I can't help but ask, what good is your pension if I'm a dead man?

NADEZHDA. But maybe they'll erect a stone monument to you for your heroism.

PAVEL. You think they would?

NADEZHDA. For heroism like that, there can't be any doubt. For the edification of future generations. You'd be like the first book printer or something.

PAVEL. You don't think people would confuse me with him?

NADEZHDA. Pavel, nobody could ever confuse you with anybody. You have a very imposing figure.

PAVEL. Then maybe I'd better not join the Party, mama.

NADEZHDA. Why not? Then what would we use to marry off Varya?

PAVEL. But, mama, you're forgetting that under the old regime I could be doomed to a martyr's death for sympathizing with the new order.

NADEZHDA. How could you possibly be doomed if you are the possessor of the dress?

PAVEL. With logic like that, under the new regime this dress and I could be doomed to a martyr's death for sympathizing with the old order.

NADEZHDA. How could you possibly be doomed if you're a party member?

PAVEL. Mama, what you are saying is that I am immortal no matter what the regime. Just think, mama. What a monument I'll be! For example, say some foreigners come to Moscow. They'll ask, "Where are the finest sights in your city?" "Right here," people will say. Then they'll ask, "Who is this, Peter the Great?" And they'll say, "No. Raise your sights a little higher. This is Pavel Sergeyevich Gulyachkin."

SCENE FOURTEEN

(Enter Varvara)

VARVARA. The dress fits Nastya perfectly.
NADEZHDA. You don't say. Where is she?
VARVARA. She's coming.
PAVEL. What if a real empress was coming out right now? How would we greet her? "Hello"? or "My compliments"?
NADEZHDA. One doesn't say "hello" to an empress. One says "Hurrah!"
VARVARA. And what do we call her? "Queen Mother"?
NADEZHDA. Only Mothers of God are called "Mother." Empresses are called "Your Majesties."
VARVARA. Are you coming?
VOICE OF NASTYA. I'll be right there.
PAVEL. It's only our cook and my knees are already shaking.

SCENE FIFTEEN

(Enter Nastya in the empress's dress and carrying a fan)

THE THREE GULYACHKINS. Hurrah, Your Majesty!
NADEZHDA. She looks so real. It's amazing how real she looks.
VARVARA. Mama, I'm getting stomach cramps from so much luxury.
PAVEL. Nastya, sweetheart, walk around the room. We'd like to get a glimpse of your other side.
VARVARA. Oh, Nastya. You simply walk without the slightest bit of taste. When I saw an English queen at the Maly Theater once, she moved across the floor exclusively like this. *(Demonstrates)*
PAVEL. Go on, Nastya, try it.
NADEZHDA. Do something with her train. Her train is dragging on the ground.
PAVEL. Allow me, mama. *(Carries her train)*
NADEZHDA. She looks so real. It's amazing how real she looks.
PAVEL. If only I'd had something like this to grab onto in peacetime, I would have gone a long way, mama.
VARVARA. Pavel, seat her on the throne.
PAVEL. Please be seated, Your Majesty. *(Seats Nastya on the chair)*
NADEZHDA. She looks so real. It's amazing how real she looks.
VARVARA. If we seated a real empress on the throne, mama, they'd be sure to give us a grocery store.
PAVEL. They'd make me prime minister.
NADEZHDA. Maybe a policeman at least, Pavel. Because doing business

with your own policeman on your side is a good thing. It's legal and profitable.

NASTYA. What am I sitting on?

PAVEL. A throne, Your Majesty.

NADEZHDA. Help! Every man for himself!

PAVEL and VARVARA. What happened?

NASTYA. What's wrong, madame?

NADEZHDA. Nastya, don't move. In the name of Christ, I invoke you, don't move. Because you are sitting on a loaded pistol.

NASTYA. A pistol? Citizens! Murder!

NADEZHDA. Nastya, don't squirm!

PAVEL. Nastya, sit there like a stunned bird or you'll kill us and yourself too.

VARVARA. Nastya, if you so much as budge, it'll shoot.

NASTYA. Heavens, I'm done for.

NADEZHDA. Don't move, I tell you!

PAVEL. Nastya, can you feel with the spot that you're sitting on which direction it's pointed in?

NASTYA. Pavel Sergeyevich, every spot on me has gone numb from terror.

PAVEL. Mama, I can't exist under the conditions of a fire attack. We're going to have to move to another apartment.

NASTYA. But Pavel Sergeyevich, you can't leave me all alone riding side saddle on a pistol.

NADEZHDA. Nastya, quit shivering! Nastya, don't shiver, because there are still seven bullets in there.

VARVARA. If only we knew which direction it might fire.

NASTYA. Oh my God! I think I just felt the trigger with something.

PAVEL. Everybody, under the chair! Dive under the chair! When it shoots, it won't shoot down, it'll shoot straight out.

(They crawl under the chair)

NASTYA. If you bump the chair with anything, I'll explode.

PAVEL. Mama, you're to blame for all of this.

NADEZHDA. No, it's Varya's fault, Pavlusha. "Let's seat her on the throne," she says. Well, she's sitting pretty now.

PAVEL. At the present moment, mama, she's sitting on all our heads.

NASTYA. Ah!

THE THREE GULYACHKINS. Oh!

PAVEL. Mama, have them bury me ceremoniously with music. After all, I'm dying under the yoke of the monarchy.

(The doorbell rings)

NADEZHDA. Heavens, someone is at the door.

VARVARA. It's probably Mister Smetanich.

NADEZHDA. Holy Saints, what are we going to do?

PAVEL. Nastya, sweetheart, while we are still sitting under you under the chair, try to get up as carefully as you can. If the pistol fires, maybe it'll miss.

NASTYA. What if it fires?! Get another pistol and shoot me if you want, but I'm not budging off of this one.

NADEZHDA. Oh, my Lord. The doorbell again.

VARVARA. Mama, what are we going to do?

NADEZHDA. Cover her up with something, quick. Throw something over her and I'll go open the door. (Leaves)

SCENE SIXTEEN

PAVEL. Varya, drag a curtain over here. Or make it a rug.

NASTYA. Pavel Sergeyevich, I think I'm beginning to detect the smell of gun powder wafting up from under me.

PAVEL. Cover her up good! Tighter, wrap it tighter!

NASTYA. Oh! I'm suffocating.

VARVARA. Well, suffocate if you have to. Only don't move!

SCENE SEVENTEEN

(Enter Nadezhda, Olimp and his son Valerian)

NADEZHDA. This way, Olimp Valerianovich. Right this way.

OLIMP. What have we here, Nadezhda Petrovna? Your dining room?

NADEZHDA. Yes, yes, Olimp Valerianovich. This is our dining room. And this is my daughter Varya.

OLIMP. I'm charmed to meet you, mademoiselle.

VARVARA. Oh, it's nothing. Nonsense, really.

OLIMP. Valerian.

VALERIAN. Yes, papa.

OLIMP. Say hello to Varvara Sergeyevna.

VALERIAN. I'm charmed.

VARVARA. Oh, you don't mean it.

NASTYA. A-choo!

ALL. Ah!

OLIMP. What seems to be the problem, Nadezhda Petrovna?

NADEZHDA. I'm dying.

OLIMP. What do you mean, you're dying? You mean, really?

NADEZHDA. Yes…, that is…, no. Pardon me, I… I think I'm all better now.

VALERIAN. I have the distinct impression that someone sneezed in here.

NADEZHDA. Oh, how could you, Valerian Olimpovich? My children are well-bred. They would never allow themselves such a thing.

VALERIAN. A-choo.

NADEZHDA. That is, I mean to say that one can pass the time quite pleasantly even when sneezing.

VARVARA. Mama, look. He's standing right next to the chair.

NADEZHDA. Varya, shut up while nobody's noticed anything. Olimp Valerianovich, I would like you to meet my communist son, Pavlusha.

OLIMP. Aha. So you have already joined the Party, have you, young man? When was it that you joined?

PAVEL. Well, you see, it was, uh, nineteen, I think, o-five... that I started thinking, that is to say, I had the impulse, because as our beloved teacher Engels said...

OLIMP. What did he say?

PAVEL. It, uh... he, uh.... Well, in a word, he said a great deal and one would never be able to remember it all.

OLIMP. Well, tell me, young man, how was it that you joined the Party? Out of convictions, or was it, uh...

PAVEL. That, I don't know. How did it happen, mama?

NADEZHDA. Olimp Valerianovich, this boy of mine is truly a wonder, he's capable of doing anything in any way you can possibly imagine.

OLIMP. I see. But tell me, young man, do you have a protege?

PAVEL. A protege?

OLIMP. A protege. Well, how does one put it? An obliging boss?

PAVEL. Obliging?

OLIMP. Well, yes. That is to say, a boss who, shall we say, has dinner at your house and will definitely find the proper occasion to return the favor.

NADEZHDA. Pavel knows Utkin himself, Olimp Valerianovich.

OLIMP. Who is Utkin?

NADEZHDA. A very famous person, Olimp Valerianovich. Just imagine, he has three communist relatives.

PAVEL. They promised to come see us today, Olimp Valerianovich.

OLIMP. They're coming here? Valerian.

VALERIAN. Yes, papa.

OLIMP. Pin your air force pin to your jacket this minute. And do what you can not to express your convictions.

VALERIAN. No problem with the pin, but as for the convictions, I don't have any. I'm an anarchist.

OLIMP. Children in our circle, Nadezhda Petrovna, always say what they shouldn't, because they repeat what they hear their parents say. However, do tell me, Nadezhda Petrovna, why is it that you keep a rug here instead of spreading it on the floor?

NADEZHDA. Don't touch it, Olimp Valerianovich. I beg you not to touch it.

OLIMP. Why is that, Nadezhda Petrovna?

NADEZHDA. It…, it…, it… is very dirty and then…, won't you please follow me into the other room, Olimp Valerianovich?

OLIMP. Valerian.

VALERIAN. Yes, papa.

OLIMP. Engage Varvara Sergeyevna in conversation. I'll be right back. Shall we go, Nadezhda Petrovna? After you, Pavel Sergeyevich.

PAVEL. Oh, no. I wouldn't think of it. You go first and I'll just tag along somehow.

(Nadezhda, Olimp and Pavel leave)

SCENE EIGHTEEN

VALERIAN. Tell me, mademoiselle, do you play the piano?

VARVARA. I never seem to have had the occasion to.

VALERIAN. Perhaps, mademoiselle, you have taken note of what the Soviet government has done to the arts?

VARVARA. Oh, you'll have to forgive me. I haven't noticed.

VALERIAN. Just imagine, it has taken free professionals and turned them into cabbies.

VARVARA. Oh, what a shame.

VALERIAN. I don't say that in an imagistic sense, but in the sense of the rent they now charge for apartments.

NASTYA. It's going to shoot.

VALERIAN. What happened? Who said it's going to shoot?

VARVARA. That, uh…, was me.

VALERIAN. You? Who's shooting who?

VARVARA. I, uh…, you see, I…, I have this shooting pain in my back.

VALERIAN. In your back? Well, mademoiselle, how do you find Einstein's theory of relativity?

VARVARA. Oh, it played at our local theater. Only Pavel told me it was just a travelogue without much of a story.

VALERIAN. Do you often go to the movies?

VARVARA. On the contrary. I find it awkward to go often.

VALERIAN. Awkward? Why is that?

VARVARA. It's dark and there are a lot of strange men there.

VALERIAN. Wait a minute. Who is that sniffling?

VARVARA. Valerian Olimpovich.

VALERIAN. What?

VARVARA. I…, I…, I meant to say…

VALERIAN. What did you mean to say?

VARVARA. That is, I…, I…, I meant to ask…

VALERIAN. What did you mean to ask?

VARVARA. Lord, what am I going to ask him? Well, then…, you…, you…
don't seem to wear a pince-nez.

VALERIAN. No. I have very healthy eyes.

VARVARA. Oh, what a shame. A pince-nez is very becoming to a man.

VALERIAN. Listen. Somebody is sniffling again.

VARVARA. That was…, that was me.

VALERIAN. You?

VARVARA. Shall we go into the living room, Valerian Olimpovich?

VALERIAN. Maybe we should remain here in the dining room, Varvara
Sergeyevna.

VARVARA. For goodness sake, let's go into the living room, Valerian
Olimpovich.

VALERIAN. In that case, allow me to offer you my hand, mademoiselle.

VARVARA. My, but you do work quickly, Valerian Olimpovich. I'm
ashamed to think of it. However, I accept.

VALERIAN. You have misunderstood me, Varvara Sergeyevna.

VARVARA. Nothing of the sort, Valerian Olimpovich. I understand you
perfectly well. But perhaps you ought to negotiate with my mother first.

VALERIAN. That's what's called getting stuck like a pig. (Leaves)

SCENE NINETEEN

VARVARA. Oh, what an impossibly passionate man he is!

SCENE TWENTY

(Enter Nadezhda and Pavel)

NADEZHDA. Varvara, why did you let Valerian Olimpovich out of your
clutches?

VARVARA. But mama, he just made me a proposal.

NADEZHDA. Varya, why are you such a shameless liar?

VARVARA. Honest, mama, I'm not a liar. "Allow me," he said, "to offer you
my hand, mademoiselle."

NADEZHDA. That's what he said?

VARVARA. That's what he said.

PAVEL. What is Nastya up to?

VARVARA. She's sniffling and sneezing.

PAVEL. Nastya, what are you sneezing for?

NASTYA. How do you expect me not to sneeze when you buried me in a dusty rug?

NADEZHDA. Bear with us a little longer. They'll be gone soon.

VARVARA. Only don't move! Don't move!

SCENE TWENTY-ONE

(Enter the Janitor)

JANITOR. Hello, comrades.

THE THREE GULYACHKINS. Hello, comrade.

JANITOR. So. Well, uh, Pavel Sergeyevich, they want you to put in an appearance at the house committee meeting.

PAVEL. The meeting?

NADEZHDA. What is the meeting about?

JANITOR. It's uh, well, it's about our trash, comrade. See, they uh, want to know when it should be hauled away. This week or next?

PAVEL. Mama, hand me my briefcase. I can't shirk my social duties. I'll go.

VARVARA. Trash. There's a fine social duty for you.

PAVEL. Varya, we just vote about it. It's others who will have to haul it away.

(Leaves with the Janitor)

NADEZHDA. Lock the door after them, Varya!

(Nadezhda and Varvara leave)

SCENE TWENTY-TWO

(Enter Olimp and Valerian)

VALERIAN. So, what you're saying, papa, is that you insist I marry this little peasant?

OLIMP. First of all, she is not a little peasant and second of all, circumstances are making the demand, not I.

VALERIAN. What do you mean she's not a peasant? She uses vegetable oil for perfume.

OLIMP. Nonsense. She'll air out in a day or two.

VALERIAN. Perhaps. But do you consider it decent that she has shooting back pains?

OLIMP. Well, if she were noisy about it, I could understand your reservations. But you won't have to worry about that.

VALERIAN. But she's not from our circle. She's no match for me.

OLIMP. You forget. Her brother is a perfect match for you. He's in the Party.

VALERIAN. Maybe, but his party is no match for us, either.

OLIMP. Valerian.

VALERIAN. Yes, papa.

OLIMP. It's time for you to get acquainted with life.

VALERIAN. Papa, you say that as if we were a family without means.

OLIMP. That's the point. In the old days, we were a family of means and everybody feared us. These days we are still a family of means, which is why we are afraid of everybody. We've got to put an end to that, and I have found just the means.

VALERIAN. What's that, papa?

OLIMP. We shall obtain our very own communist.

VALERIAN. How do you do that, papa?

OLIMP. It depends on you, Valerian.

VALERIAN. On me?

OLIMP. Yes, Valerian. Didn't you know that Nadezhda Petrovna is offering Pavel Sergeyevich as a dowry for her daughter?

VALERIAN. What good could someone like him be of?

OLIMP. Oh, come now. A person like Pavel Sergeyevich isn't a person at all. He's a whole insurance policy. If I need someone to vouch for me, he'll vouch for me. If I need someone to intercede for me, he'll intercede for me. If I need someone to recommend me, he'll recommend me. If I need someone to shine my shoes, he'll shine my shoes.

SCENE TWENTY-THREE

(Enter Nadezhda and Varvara)

NADEZHDA. Have a seat at the table, Olimp Valerianovich. Please have a seat.

VARVARA. The doorbell.

NADEZHDA. That's probably the communists.

ALL. The communists?

NADEZHDA. Varya, get the sturgeon pie off the table and I'll go peek through the peep-hole. (Leaves)

SCENE TWENTY-FOUR

OLIMP. Valerian.

VALERIAN. Yes, papa.

OLIMP. Look at me. I don't look too decent, do I?

VALERIAN. No, papa. You look just like you always do.
OLIMP. Valerian.
VALERIAN. Yes, papa.
OLIMP. Straighten up the pin on your jacket and sing something in a revolutionary spirit.
VALERIAN. What do you want me to sing?
OLIMP. A song. Any song. For instance, "You Fell a Martyred Victim."

SCENE TWENTY-FIVE

(Enter Nadezhda)

NADEZHDA. That's who it is, the communists. Varya, quick, turn over "Evening in Copenhagen" and I'll turn over "I Believe in Thee, O Lord."
VARVARA. Mama, all of my insides are turning over upside down from terror.
NADEZHDA. I don't give a damn about your insides. These days our whole life is turning upside down. Saints alive! They're ringing again. Quick, Varya, get the bottles out of here and I'll go open the door. What will be will be.
OLIMP. Wait, Nadezhda Petrovna. That is no work for a woman. You step into the next room and Valerian and I will receive them together.
NADEZHDA. The Lord be with you, Olimp Valerianovich. If you need me, call me. God be willing, Pavlusha will be here soon.

(Nadezhda and Varvara leave)

SCENE TWENTY-SIX

OLIMP. Valerian.
VALERIAN. Yes, papa.
OLIMP. Wait for me here. *(Leaves)*

(Valerian sings)

SCENE TWENTY-SEVEN

(Enter Olimp, the Hurdy-Gurdy Man, the Drummer and the Woman with a Parrot and Tambourine)

OLIMP. Comrades, be so kind. Come in, come in, please. Valerian.
VALERIAN. Yes, papa.

OLIMP. Why aren't you singing?

VALERIAN. My song is already sung.

DRUMMER. Are these the communists we're playing relatives for?

HURDY-GURDY MAN. Probably. Look, that one has a pin.

OLIMP. Sit down, comrades. Please do sit down. Pavel Sergeyevich will be here any minute.

HURDY-GURDY MAN. Pavel Sergeyevich? He's Pavlusha to me, my good man. Simply Pavlusha.

OLIMP. Then you have known him for a long time, have you, comrade?

HURDY-GURDY MAN. How could I possibly not know him, my good man, when I am his own dear uncle?

VALERIAN. You are his uncle?

HURDY-GURDY MAN. From the very moment of his birth. You know, I used to finish my shift at the factory and make a beeline to go see him. He'd always be sitting there on his mother's knee and sucking at his mother's breast. So I'd make horns behind my head with my fingers, like this, and I'd say, "Pavlusha! Do you love the working class?" He'd quit sucking instantly and say, "I do, uncle! Oh, how I love it!" And then he'd start shivering all over.

WOMAN WITH A PARROT AND TAMBOURINE. That boy was so politically conscious from his very childhood, there's no way you could even describe it.

OLIMP. You know him from childhood, too?

WOMAN WITH A PARROT AND TAMBOURINE. My dear, what do you expect when I am his favorite aunt?

VALERIAN. My bride's relatives are all idiots.

WOMAN WITH A PARROT AND TAMBOURINE. Whenever we'd go walking past a factory, he always tried breaking in through the walls with his little hands.

OLIMP. Pardon me, comrades, but I've got to leave you for a moment. Valerian!

VALERIAN. Yes, papa.

OLIMP. I can't believe that Nadezhda Petrovna didn't tell us that her relatives are these communists. We've got to go find her.

(Olimp and Valerian leave)

SCENE TWENTY-EIGHT

WOMAN WITH A PARROT AND TAMBOURINE. I think we poured it on good and thick.

DRUMMER. I'll say. And now it wouldn't be a bad idea to pour a little down the hatch.

HURDY-GURDY MAN. Here's the girl.

SCENE TWENTY-NINE

(Enter Varvara)

VARVARA. You're here already?
DRUMMER. Yes, ma'am. We're here, all right.
VARVARA. Where are the communists?
DRUMMER. We already gave them a working over, miss. So now we can move on to the sturgeon pie.
VARVARA. Just a minute. Mama will be right here. *(Leaves)*

SCENE THIRTY

(Enter Nadezhda)

NADEZHDA. Hello, comrades.
ALL. Hello, madame.
NADEZHDA. Did you comrades have a nice chat with Valerian Olimpovich?
HURDY-GURDY MAN. I'd say we had a first-class chat. And now it would be a good idea to wet the whistle.
NADEZHDA. I'll bring you some water right away, comrades.
HURDY-GURDY MAN. Water? What water? Are you trying to make fun of us, madame?
NADEZHDA. What makes you think I would dare make fun of you, comrades?
HURDY-GURDY MAN. Listen, madame, produce what we agreed on. First of all, sturgeon pie, and then a bottle for each of us.
NADEZHDA. What are you talking about, comrades? We never have sturgeon pie and, as for wine, I've never even set eyes on it. I've heard about it, but I've never had occasion to cross its path.
HURDY-GURDY MAN. You've never crossed its path?
NASTYA. Ow! You stepped on my corn.
HURDY-GURDY MAN. What was that?
NASTYA. Don't touch me or I'll shoot.
ALL. Help! Murder!

(The doorbell rings)

NADEZHDA. Oh, my God. We're done for now.

SCENE THIRTY-ONE

(Enter Varvara)

VARVARA. Mama, it's Tamara Leopoldovna.
NADEZHDA. Tamara Leopoldovna? Help, I'm dying.
VARVARA. Gentlemen, go into the other room. Go into the other room.

(The Hurdy-Gurdy Man, the Drummer and the Woman with a Parrot and Tambourine leave)

SCENE THIRTY-TWO

NADEZHDA. Nastya! Get up off that chair this instant!
NASTYA. Kill me if you want. But I'm not budging.
VARVARA. Nastya, even if it fires, it won't hurt you where it's aimed.
NASTYA. I can't, Varvara Sergeyevna, as God is my witness, I can't.
NADEZHDA. Varya! Bring two buckets of water!

(Varvara runs out)

SCENE THIRTY-THREE

NASTYA. What's the water for, madame?
NADEZHDA. We'll soak the gun powder under you. They say that wet guns don't shoot. Oh my God! The doorbell again.

SCENE THIRTY-FOUR

(Enter Varvara with buckets)

NADEZHDA. Bring 'em over here! Quick! Quick! Right here. Now, pour them under Nastya.
NASTYA. Madame! I'm drowning!
VARVARA. Nastya, breathe with your nose and you won't drown.
NASTYA. Help! I'm drowning! I'm drowning!
NADEZHDA. It's probably damp by now. Nastya, get up! Grab her by the arms! Grab her by the arms! There. Now, crawl in the trunk!
NASTYA. Why the trunk?
NADEZHDA. Crawl in the trunk, when you're told to crawl in the trunk!
NASTYA. But madame, I'm all wet.
NADEZHDA. You can dry out in there.

(They put her in the trunk)

Bend your head. Come on, bend it. Varvara, close the trunk and I'll go open the door for Tamara Leopoldovna. *(Leaves)*

(Varvara closes the trunk and leaves)

SCENE THIRTY-FIVE

(Enter Nadezhda and Tamara)

TAMARA. I have been so worried, so worried! Tell me, nothing has happened to it, has it?
NADEZHDA. Rest assured, Tamara Leopoldovna. It's all in one piece.
TAMARA. Oh, show me, Nadezhda Petrovna!
NADEZHDA. Do you mean you don't trust me, Tamara Leopoldovna?
TAMARA. Oh, I'm a bundle of nerves, Nadezhda Petrovna!
NADEZHDA. There are too many strangers around, Tamara Leopoldovna. But look, a tip of it is sticking out here. See?
TAMARA. Oh, what happiness! I have been so worried, so worried!

SCENE THIRTY-SIX

(Enter Ivan)

IVAN. Police! Police! Police!
NADEZHDA. Ivan Ivanovich, what gives you the right to express yourself like that in a dining room? People eat here, they don't express themselves.
IVAN. You're fancy intonations aren't going to help you now. The police will be here any minute.
TAMARA. Help! The police!

SCENE THIRTY-SEVEN

(Enter the Drummer, the Hurdy-Gurdy Man, the Woman with a Parrot and Tambourine, Valerian, Olimp and Varvara)

DRUMMER. Who said, "police"?
HURDY-GURDY MAN. The police?
WOMAN WITH A PARROT AND TAMBOURINE. What police?
VALERIAN. What happened?
OLIMP. What is going on?

NADEZHDA. Ivan Ivanovich, I'll get help from a friendlier precinct.
IVAN. There isn't a soul in the whole republic who can help you now.
VALERIAN. Who is this?
TAMARA. He's probably a commissar. Look at his hat.
VARVARA. Maestro, play! That's the neighbor we're driving out.
HURDY-GURDY MAN. Hit it, men!

(Music plays. Everyone except Tamara and Valerian leaves, shouting: "Police! Police! Police! Help! Help! Help! Play! Play! Play!")

SCENE THIRTY-EIGHT

TAMARA. Young man, do you believe in God?
VALERIAN. Approximately.
TAMARA. Save a helpless woman! Carry away this trunk!
VALERIAN. This trunk? What's in it?
TAMARA. Young man, I'll tell you a state secret. This trunk contains everything that is left of Russia in Russia.
VALERIAN. In that case, it can't be very heavy.
TAMARA. I implore you. Save it or all is lost.
VALERIAN. All right. I'll try.
TAMARA. We only have to make it as far as my cab.

(Tamara and Valerian carry out the trunk)

SCENE THIRTY-NINE

(Varvara, Nadezhda, Olimp, Ivan, the Hurdy-Gurdy Man, the Drummer and the Woman with a Parrot and Tambourine all return. They are all dancing to music)

VARVARA. Play! Play harder! Dance, gentlemen, dance! We're driving him out.
IVAN. So you're frightened, are you, Nadezhda Petrovna? Do you think there are no laws in the Soviet Republic? There are, Nadezhda Petrovna, there are. There isn't a country on earth that lets you drown a man in milk and macaroni. Nadezhda Petrovna, do you really think I won't be able to bring you to justice just because you pray with a grammophone? These days, even a grammophone can be convicted of counterrevolutionary activities.
OLIMP. You ought to keep it down about counterrevolutionaries, comrade. Her son is a communist.
IVAN. A communist? Then let him swear on a Bible at the police station that

he is a communist.

OLIMP. What is the meaning of this, Nadezhda Petrovna?

NADEZHDA. Well, it seems that he hasn't quite joined officially yet. But he definitely will, Olimp Valerianovich.

OLIMP. He hasn't joined yet? Are you telling me that you deceived me, Nadezhda Petrovna? You are downright seditious, Nadezhda Petrovna.

IVAN. That's right. Seditious.

OLIMP. Where is your dowry, Nadezhda Petrovna?

HURDY-GURDY MAN. Where is the sturgeon pie, Nadezhda Petrovna?

DRUMMER. You're a liar, Nadezhda Petrovna.

WOMAN WITH A PARROT AND TAMBOURINE. You're a crook, Nadezhda Petrovna.

IVAN. You're a typical landlord, Nadezhda Petrovna. That's what you are.

SCENE FORTY

(Enter Pavel)

PAVEL. Silence! I'm a party member!

IVAN. You can't frighten me with that, now, Pavel Sergeyevich.

PAVEL. I can't frighten you, huh? And what if I'm Lunacharsky's[2] drinking buddy?

IVAN. What kind of communist are you, Pavel Sergeyevich? You don't even have any documents. There is no such thing as a communist without documents.

PAVEL. A document? You want a document?

IVAN. You don't have any, Pavel Sergeyevich.

PAVEL. I don't?

IVAN. You don't.

PAVEL. How about a warrant?

IVAN. You don't have a warrant either.

PAVEL. I don't? Then what's this?

IVAN. A warrant.

(Everyone runs out)

PAVEL. Mama, hold me back or I'll use this warrant to arrest all of Russia.

SCENE FORTY-ONE

NADEZHDA. Oh my God. The trunk is gone.

---

[2] Anatoly Lunacharsky was the first People's Commissar of Enlightenment.

48

PAVEL. The trunk?

NADEZHDA. Pavlusha, the dress was in the trunk.

VARVARA. Yes, mama. And Nastya was in the dress.

PAVEL. Mama, what do you need a dress for when I have a warrant?

NADEZHDA. Pavel, you mean you really have a warrant?

PAVEL. Read it, mama, and you'll see.

NADEZHDA. "War-rant." Oh! I'd better not.

PAVEL. Read it, mama. Read it.

NADEZHDA. *(Reads)* "These presents have been presented to Pavel Sergeyevich Gulyachkin as proof that he does, in fact, live in the apartment he lives in. Official signature and seal affixed by..."

PAVEL. Read on, mama. Read on.

NADEZHDA. "...by the Chairman of the Housing Committee, Pavel Sergeyevich Gulyachkin."

PAVEL. A carbon copy has been sent to comrade Stalin.

END OF ACT II

ACT III

(A room in the Smetanich apartment)

SCENE ONE

AVTONOM. Agafangel, where is my copy of the "Tsarist News"?

SCENE TWO

(Enter Agafangel)

AGAFANGEL. Right here, your excellency.
AVTONOM. What are you doing?
AGAFANGEL. Pardon me, your excellency.
AVTONOM. Pardon what?
AGAFANGEL. I don't know, your excellency.
AVTONOM. What do you mean you don't know?
AGAFANGEL. There's no way of knowing, your excellency.
AVTONOM. Where is my copy of the "Tsarist News"?
AGAFANGEL. It has perished, your excellency.
AVTONOM. Perished?
AGAFANGEL. Totally, your excellency. So much so, that you can't even touch it anymore.
AVTONOM. Why not?
AGAFANGEL. Because all that is left is one big hole, your excellency.
AVTONOM. A hole?
AGAFANGEL. A hole, your excellency.
AVTONOM. How could that have happened?
AGAFANGEL. A law of nature, your excellency.
AVTONOM. A law? There is no such law. For example, I'm not young any-more either, but I don't have any holes in me.
AGAFANGEL. There is no point in comparing you to a newspaper, your excellency. After all, it would seem that you are a person.
AVTONOM. Don't pull the wool over my eyes. Tell me straight. You didn't, uh..., you couldn't have, uh..., in the bathroom?
AGAFANGEL. Absolutely not, your excellency.
AVTONOM. What?
AGAFANGEL. I don't know, your excellency.

50

AVTONOM. Then why did you say "absolutely not"?

AGAFANGEL. It was just my ardor, your excellency.

AVTONOM. I'm asking you in plain Russian, were you, uh..., perhaps, reading it after me? Agafangel, you haven't taken up politics, have you?

AGAFANGEL. Your excellency, what need have I of politics when I am fully cared for?

AVTONOM. Well then, maybe you weren't as careful with it as you should have been?

AGAFANGEL. Absolutely not, your excellency. Every morning I wiped it off with a wet rag.

AVTONOM. Strange. Then how could it have perished? My, what a healthy issue it was! The print. The ideas. The letters. Why do you think that was? Because people then were great. Take Sytin, for example.[1] He published the newspaper "Russian Word." And, oh, how he did publish it! He built a three-story building and printed it on every floor. Every time you'd ride by, you'd think to yourself, "There it is. The bulwark of the Russian empire. The three-story 'Russian Word.'" Agafangel.

AGAFANGEL. Yes, your excellency.

AVTONOM. What am I going to do now?

AGAFANGEL. Allow me to make a suggestion, your excellency.

AVTONOM. What suggestion?

AGAFANGEL. "The World Illustrated," your excellency. They print lots of pictures.

AVTONOM. Some trashy magazine, I imagine?

AGAFANGEL. Absolutely, your excellency.

AVTONOM. Well, go on. Read it to me. I can't see without my glasses.

AGAFANGEL. From the first page, your excellency?

AVTONOM. Begin at the beginning.

AGAFANGEL. There is a portrait, your excellency.

AVTONOM. Whose?

AGAFANGEL. His Highness, the Sovereign Emperor, your excellency.

AVTONOM. Attention! Give me my glasses. Where did you get this?

AGAFANGEL. In the bathroom, your excellency.

AVTONOM. Was there anybody else in there?

AGAFANGEL. There was, your excellency.

AVTONOM. Who?

AGAFANGEL. King Albert of Belgium. He was painted in among his subjects, your excellency.

AVTONOM. Where is he now?

AGAFANGEL. No sooner did I finish looking at him, I used him, your excellency.

---

[1] Ivan Sytin was a prominent Russian publisher before 1917.

AVTONOM. Ah, a genuine martyr king. Hand me my handkerchief and read on.

AGAFANGEL. The commander-in-chief, Tsar Nikolai Nikolayevich, standing amidst a hurricane of enemy fire, is eating cabbage soup out of a common soldier's pot.

AVTONOM. Where are heroes like that now? Just think what an example he set. Every moment on the threshold of death, but he didn't flinch even when eating cabbage soup under a hurricane of enemy fire. What do you say to that, huh?

AGAFANGEL. Absolutely, your excellency. He could easily have died. Soldier's slop is worse than any poison known to man, your excellency.

AVTONOM. Agafangel.

AGAFANGEL. Yes, your excellency.

AVTONOM. Mix up some glue this instant. We have to glue these portraits to some heavy cardboard. One has to have a sense of responsibility. Otherwise, the commander-in-chief might be replaced by a hole.

AGAFANGEL. Right away, your excellency.

AVTONOM. Wait a minute. When you glue them to the cardboard, dry them out. And then bring them to me mornings with my coffee. I'll read them. I just can't live without politics. All my life I took an interest in politics every morning. Now go!

(Agafangel leaves)

SCENE THREE

(Enter Anatoly)

ANATOLY. You won't believe what interesting news I've got! You won't believe what interesting news I've got!

AVTONOM. What news?

ANATOLY. It turns out that there is no God.

AVTONOM. What do you mean?

ANATOLY. Simple. There's no such thing.

AVTONOM. In that case, young man, will you please tell me who has replaced Him?

ANATOLY. Hydrogen.

AVTONOM. What?

ANATOLY. Well, basically, gases of all kinds.

AVTONOM. Who told you that?

ANATOLY. At school they gave us a lecture with all kinds of strange pictures, uncle. And they showed us that there is no God anymore.

AVTONOM. No God. In that case, young man, you might tell me what everything we can see comes out of?

ANATOLY. Nature.

AVTONOM. Aha, and what did nature come out of?

ANATOLY. The air.

AVTONOM. Aha, and what did the air come out of?

ANATOLY. From…, I don't know….

AVTONOM. Aha! "I don't know!" It came out of God!

ANATOLY. But uncle, if all the air came out of God, then it's really true that he doesn't exist.

AVTONOM. Anatoly.

ANATOLY. Yes, uncle.

AVTONOM. You will not be going to school anymore.

ANATOLY. Hurray! No more school.

AVTONOM. You aren't a little boy anymore, Anatoly. It's time for you to become a person.

ANATOLY. What kind of person, uncle?

AVTONOM. What kind of person? Agafangel.

SCENE FOUR

(Enter Agafangel)

AGAFANGEL. Yes, your excellency.

AVTONOM. Unveil it!

(Agafangel removes a sheet from a mannequin of a general in full regalia)

AVTONOM. That is the kind of person you'll become.

ANATOLY. How can I do that, uncle?

AVTONOM. Under my tutelage, it will be easy. At-ten-tion! You just wait. The old days will return.

ANATOLY. Uncle, when will the old days come back to us?

AVTONOM. When will they come back to us? We have to go back to them.

ANATOLY. Then let's go as quick as possible, uncle.

AVTONOM. Left! Right! Left! Meanwhile, I'll just sit awhile. I get tired, you know. Age. Agafangel.

AGAFANGEL. Yes, your excellency.

AVTONOM. Sing!

(Agafangel and Anatoly march and sing)

Oh how Tsar Nikolai Nikolayevich would weep if only he could see us! Agafangel!

53

AGAFANGEL. Yes, your excellency.

AVTONOM. If you were to see the tsar right now, what would you do?

AGAFANGEL. I would weep, your excellency.

AVTONOM. That's my man.

AGAFANGEL. My pleasure, your excellency.

AVTONOM. If there were only a hundred fine men like us with the tsar leading the way.... Strange, isn't it? What's taking him so long? Where is he? Oh, how weary we are of waiting.

SCENE FIVE

(Valerian and the Cabbie carry in the trunk)

VALERIAN. Careful. Careful. Ease it down. Ease it down. There. Thank you.

(The cabbie leaves)

SCENE SIX

AVTONOM. Valerian.

VALERIAN. Yes, uncle.

AVTONOM. Why did you drag this thing in here?

VALERIAN. I did nothing of the sort.

AVTONOM. How's that?

VALERIAN. I didn't drag it anywhere. I saved it.

AVTONOM. How did you save it?

VALERIAN. You'll never be able to understand, uncle.

AVTONOM. Why not?

VALERIAN. Because I don't understand myself.

AVTONOM. Valerian, how is it that you don't understand what you yourself are doing?

VALERIAN. Uncle, I've never done anything before. I'm an anarchist. Anyway, judge for yourself. Right out of the blue, some man in a pot came running in.

AVTONOM. In a what?

VALERIAN. A pot. And he started screaming "police!" at the top of his lungs. Then a communist grabbed a drum and started beating on it with a stick.

AVTONOM. Those communists are all beasts. And then what happened?

VALERIAN. Then for some reason everybody disappeared into the other room with the guy in the pot and some strange lady fell on her knees in front of me.

AVTONOM. On her knees?

VALERIAN. Yes.

AVTONOM. Typical Soviet woman.

VALERIAN. On the contrary, uncle. She was really quite decent.

AVTONOM. Decent? What could a decent woman want with you?

VALERIAN. You see, uncle, she divulged a state secret to me.

AVTONOM. A state secret? Consisting of what?

VALERIAN. Consisting of a trunk, uncle.

AVTONOM. A trunk? What's in the trunk?

VALERIAN. This trunk contains everything that is left of Russia in Russia.

AVTONOM. Valerian, what could possibly be left?

VALERIAN. I don't know, uncle. It's locked. I thought you might tell me. After all, uncle, you're the politician in our family.

AVTONOM. What could be left of our Russia? Today there's only a hole where yesterday there was the "Tsarist News."

ANATOLY. That's just what it is, a hole.

AVTONOM. Where's there a hole?

ANATOLY. I don't know, but it's leaking.

VALERIAN. Leaking? Oh, I'll say it's leaking.

AVTONOM. Then there must be an animal of some sort or maybe a person in there.

VALERIAN. What do you think, uncle, what kind of animal or person could be left of Russia in Russia?

AVTONOM. What kind of animal or person? Well, me for instance.

VALERIAN. And what else?

AVTONOM. You. And Patriarch Tikhon is also left of Russia in Russia.

VALERIAN. He may be left of Russia, uncle, but there's nothing of Russia left in him.

AVTONOM. Y-e-s. A lot of water has gone under the bridge.

ANATOLY. There's another hole, uncle. And it's leaking too.

VALERIAN. Uncle, what if there really is a person in there? Psst! Pardon me, are you a person?

VOICE OF NASTYA. No. I'm a woman.

ALL. A woman!

VALERIAN. Uncle, what woman could be left from Russia?

AVTONOM. A colonel I know once told me that he met one of the grand duchesses on a beach in the Crimea.

VALERIAN. Which one, uncle?

AVTONOM. Anastasiya Nikolayevna, Valerian. Only, somehow I don't believe it. The colonel was near-sighted from birth. Once he even confused himself with a general.

VALERIAN. Even so, uncle, we've got to find out. Listen, please don't consider me rude, but what is your name?

VOICE OF NASTYA. Nastya.

VALERIAN. What?

VOICE OF NASTYA. Anastasiya.

ALL. It's her!

AVTONOM. My God, it's her. Lord, what are we going to do?

VALERIAN. Maybe it's a different Anastasiya. I'll ask her a question.

AVTONOM. "I'll ask her a question," he says. If it is the grand duchess, how are you going to do that? There's nothing in the regulation book concerning a situation like this.

VALERIAN. I'll ask her a question as if I don't know anything. Oh, by the way, mademoiselle, what was your father's name?

VOICE OF NASTYA. Nikolai.

AVTONOM. Agafangel.

AGAFANGEL. Yes, Avtonom Sigismundovich.

AVTONOM. Hold me!

SCENE SEVEN

(Enter Olimp)

OLIMP. Gentlemen, I hear there are rumblings against Soviet power in Poland again.

AVTONOM. Who cares about Poland when you don't even know what is going on in your own home?

OLIMP. I don't understand.

VALERIAN. Pardon me, papa, but I saved Russia.

OLIMP. How did you save Russia?

VALERIAN. Absolutely by chance.

AVTONOM. Olimp, he saved one of the grand duchesses.

OLIMP. What?

AVTONOM. It's true, Olimp.

VALERIAN. Anastasiya Nikolayevna, papa.

OLIMP. Anastasiya Nikolayevna? It can't be.

VALERIAN. How can't it be when she said so herself?

OLIMP. But where is she then?

AVTONOM. Right here, Olimp. In the trunk.

OLIMP. In the trunk? Then we've got to liberate her.

AVTONOM. We have to arrange a proper reception.

VALERIAN. A reception? One second, uncle. *(Leaves)*

SCENE EIGHT

OLIMP. Are you sure you're not mistaken, gentlemen? Are you certain it's her?

AVTONOM. Why do you think they would be keeping a live woman under lock and key if she wasn't a duchess or something?

SCENE NINE

(Valerian returns with a roll of French bread and some salt)

AVTONOM. Valerian.

VALERIAN. Yes, uncle.

AVTONOM. What is that for?

VALERIAN. It's bread and salt for an official reception. Unfortunately, the bread is a day old.

AVTONOM. However, fortunately it's French bread. I think she'll like that. After all, Valerian, the only true Russian patriots left are all French. Stand over here, Valerian. Anatoly, grab a flower. It will be more ceremonious.

ANATOLY. Will a cactus do, uncle?

AVTONOM. Oh Lord, what a moment! Just think, our entire future is about to rise before our eyes!

ANATOLY. Uncle, open it up quickly. Otherwise she's going to drip out entirely.

AVTONOM. Are you ready, gentlemen?

All. Ready.

AVTONOM. Here we go.

VALERIAN. Do you realize what you are opening, uncle?

AVTONOM. What?

VALERIAN. A new page in history.

AVTONOM. Agafangel.

AGAFANGEL. Yes, Avtonom Sigismundovich.

AVTONOM. Line the route. Attention! *(Opens the trunk)*

NASTYA. *(Crawling out)* Where am I?

AVTONOM. Among loyal subjects, Your Highness.

NASTYA. Sir, you are mistaken.

AVTONOM. I swear to you, Your Highness.

NASTYA. Oh, come now.

OLIMP. Believe us, Your Highness. Your Highness, if we had known that you were in Moscow all this time…

NASTYA. On the contrary. I only arrived recently.

OLIMP. Were you alone, Your Highness?

NASTYA. You seem prone to make errors all the time, sir.

OLIMP. Excuse me, Your Highness. Who were you with?

NASTYA. What a funny fellow. I was with my uncle.

AVTONOM. What! Then the Grand Duke Mikhail Alexandrovich has also returned to Moscow? Hurrah!

ALL. Hurrah!

NASTYA. Ah!

OLIMP. What is the matter, Your Highness?

NASTYA. I think I'm all wet.

VALERIAN. Papa, she doesn't feel well.

AVTONOM. Hold her! Hold her!

ANATOLY. She fell right on the cactus. Look, she's all wet.

OLIMP. We must undress her immediately or she'll catch cold.

VALERIAN. Allow me, papa.

AVTONOM. Valerian, you should be ashamed to say a thing like that. You're not a boy, anymore, Valerian.

ANATOLY. In that case, uncle, let me. I'm still a boy.

AVTONOM. Anatoly! That's enough indecency from you! I will do it. Don't forget, our task is the salvation of Russia.

VALERIAN. But uncle, it was me who saved Russia. How come others get to undress her?

AVTONOM. You saved her? How did you save her? Like a coward, in a cab. While I…

OLIMP. Avtonom, don't forget it was I who said first that we should liberate her.

ANATOLY. But papa, it was the leaky hole that led us to her and I discovered the hole.

AVTONOM. What's the hole got to do with it when I was the one?

OLIMP. No, I did it.

VALERIAN. No, I did it.

All. No, I did it.

AGAFANGEL. Avtonom Sigismundovich.

AVTONOM. What do you want?

AGAFANGEL. If you keep this up, there will soon be nothing left of her but a wet spot.

OLIMP. What are we doing, gentlemen? Carry her to bed.

(All except Olimp pick up Nastya)

AVTONOM. Just think, in the old days, it took all of Russia to carry people like this on their backs. Now, four people is more than plenty.

(They carry her out)

SCENE TEN

OLIMP. (At the telephone) If I hadn't seen her with my own eyes, I would

58

never have believed it. Five, sixteen, sixty-four, please. Thank you. Stepan Stepanovich? Stepan Stepanovich, news from the most trustworthy sources. Immediately drop whatever you're doing and start buying stocks. What? Tsarist stocks. No, no, I feel fine. I'm telling you, this comes from the most trustworthy sources. I can't. You know perfectly well there's a commissar sitting on every line. Oh, all right. I'll tell you in German, then. They're all peasants and they don't know any German. All right, listen. Just a second. Just a second. Damn! I forgot the word. I know I studied it once. Well, in a word, they've returned to Moscow... Moscow, you understand? That's right. Moscow. The gross grand Fürstin. Fürstin. The grand duchess, get it? Anastasiya Nikolayevna. In German they say that just like we do. Und..., und..., and, get it? And. Und the Grossfürst, too. It's the same thing, gross..., gross..., that means big. The grand duke, get it? Michel. Michel. Oh, come on. Mikhail, understand? That's right. Mikhail Alexandrovich. You understand me? Only please, don't tell a soul. Whew! There you have it! A good education will always come to a man's rescue.

SCENE ELEVEN

(Agafangel with the dress, Avtonom and Valerian return)

AVTONOM. Shh. Her Highness is sleeping.
OLIMP. Gentlemen, while her Highness is asleep, let's decide what we're going to do next.
VALERIAN. I think we ought to walk on tiptoe, papa.
OLIMP. And I think you ought to marry Varvara Sergeyevna instantly. Any minute now we may need to fall back on our own personal communist.
VALERIAN. All right, papa. But only on one condition.
OLIMP. What's that?
VALERIAN. Only if Varvara Sergeyevna is going to be my kept woman.
OLIMP. How can she be your kept woman if you're getting married today in a church?
VALERIAN. You misunderstood me, papa. In fact, she'll be my wife. Only I'll tell my friends that she's my kept woman so as not to feel ashamed.
OLIMP. I suppose that will be more seemly.

(The telephone rings)

Who could that be? Hello? Oh, it's you Mister Ilinkin. What? Can you trust Stepan Stepanovich? What? Stocks and bonds? Buy! Buy! Yes. In whatever quantity you can. What? Very much so. I recommend it. Yes. They've arrived. From the most trustworthy sources. It should soon be all over. Only please, don't tell a soul. Good-bye. All right Valerian, get ready and

I'll send for Nadezhda Petrovna.

(Valerian leaves. During this conversation, Agafangel carries the trunk into the next room)

SCENE TWELVE

AVTONOM. You know, Olimp, I think it would be a good idea for her Highness the Empress to change her name for awhile. Otherwise, we might not be able to get her a housing permit. What if the housing committee figured out who she is?

OLIMP. Yes. The name Romanov might attract attention.

SCENE THIRTEEN

(Enter Nadezhda)

NADEZHDA. Olimp Valerianovich, don't believe that desperado. For God's sake, don't believe him.

OLIMP. What happened, Nadezhda Petrovna?

AVTONOM. What's going on?

NADEZHDA. Olimp Valerianovich, he may have told you that he's an honest person, but that's just a smoke screen.

OLIMP. Who? I don't understand.

NADEZHDA. Ivan Ivanovich.

OLIMP. What Ivan Ivanovich?

NADEZHDA. Ivan Ivanovich Shironkin. Our boarder.

AVTONOM. What did he say?

NADEZHDA. "Nadezhda Petrovna," he says, "I know that your son is no communist because his ancestors are all parasites." I lived in full legal matrimony with my husband for nineteen years and, just imagine, this man has the nerve to tell me my son is the product of parasites. So I said, "Ivan Ivanovich, why are you spreading such a disgusting legend about my offspring?" And he says, "I can prove to any citizen that your son is a parasitic element because he doesn't work anywhere." And I said, "But why should he work anywhere when, by profession, he is unemployed?" And he said, "I don't care. I'll prove it anyway."

OLIMP. Pardon the expression, but what kind of a moron is he trying to prove things like that to?

NADEZHDA. You, Olimp Valerianovich. You. Only don't believe him, Olimp Valerianovich. For God's sake don't believe him.

OLIMP. I wouldn't even think of listening to him, Nadezhda Petrovna.

NADEZHDA. Olimp Valerianovich, who could possibly think that my Pavlusha is not a communist when, you yourself, Olimp Valerianovich, saw that he has a genuine warrant? And what a potent warrant it is! You may believe it or not, but I couldn't sleep a wink all night long. Olimp Valerianovich, I couldn't stop thinking, what if he arrests me? What if he arrests me?

AVTONOM. What are you talking about? What would he arrest his own mother for?

NADEZHDA. Avtonom Sigismundovich, you simply can't imagine what a terrible ideologue he is. He's like a drunken fool with this idea in his head, Avtonom Sigismundovich. You even come near him and he says, "I'll arrest everybody." I'm afraid he got that from his father. Whenever his father would get drunk he'd say, "Let me out of here. I want to go abroad and make mincemeat of all those Germans."

OLIMP. What for?

NADEZHDA. "Let 'em all bow down before the Russian God," he used to say.

AVTONOM. You mean your son is really that ferocious?

NADEZHDA. He's ferocious, all right, Avtonom Sigismundovich. He's ferocious. But when he's in the company of his higher-ups, Avtonom Sigismundovich, he's as gentle as a little birdie.

AVTONOM. What birdie?

NADEZHDA. A pigeon, Avtonom Sigismundovich, a pigeon. Or maybe it's a crane.

AVTONOM. Why a crane?

NADEZHDA. Because he balances on one leg, Avtonom Sigismundovich.

OLIMP. I like your son, Nadezhda Petrovna.

NADEZHDA. You know how we want to please you, Olimp Valerianovich. And as for my daughter Varya, Olimp Valerianovich, she has completely lost her appetite because of your son. It happens whenever we're at the dinner table and she starts thinking about Valerian Olimpovich, Olimp Valerianovich. Even the most tasty morsel gets stuck in her throat. And she says, "Mama, I've seen a lot of terribly handsome men, but Valerian Olimpovich is the most terrible of them all."

OLIMP. In that case, Nadezhda Petrovna, why put off the wedding?

NADEZHDA. My dear Olimp Valerianovich, you mean you've decided?

OLIMP. I want to do it today, Nadezhda Petrovna. Today. Only there is one small condition.

NADEZHDA. What condition is that, Olimp Valerianovich?

OLIMP. Nadezhda Petrovna, I want your son to move in with us today.

NADEZHDA. Oh, Olimp Valerianovich, our whole family is planning to move in with you.

OLIMP. What? Don't frighten me like that, Nadezhda Petrovna. No, why would you want to do that?

NADEZHDA. Don't worry, Olimp Valerianovich. It will be no problem at all. We'll just pack up our things and head on over.

OLIMP. He doesn't need any things, Nadezhda Petrovna. All he needs is his warrant.

NADEZHDA. Olimp Valerianovich, he never so much as takes a step without his warrant. This morning when he came home from the bath-house he said, "I took my whole bath with my scrub brush in my right hand and my warrant in my left hand. Let everybody see I'm a bigwig even when I'm naked."

OLIMP. I see. Well, we'll be expecting you, Nadezhda Petrovna.... Listen, Avtonom, could you.... God be with you, Nadezhda Petrovna, it's time for you to go.

NADEZHDA. I'm going, Olimp Valerianovich. I'm going.

OLIMP. Can't you do it a little more quickly, Nadezhda Petrovna?

NADEZHDA. In a flash, Olimp Valerianovich. In a flash. Just like a... horse.
(Leaves)

SCENE FOURTEEN

OLIMP. What is it, Avtonom?

AVTONOM. *(At the telephone)* It's Zarkhin, Olimp.

OLIMP. What does he want?

AVTONOM. He recommends you buy up stocks, Olimp.

OLIMP. What stocks?

AVTONOM. "What stocks," he says. Tsarist? He says Tsarist stocks, Olimp. Yes, yes. I hear you. Olimp, he says... who arrived? Who? Who arrived? The Grand Duke Mikhail Alexandrovich? The Grand Duke Mikhail Alexandrovich has arrived in Moscow. What? What? Olimp! Anastasiya Nikolayevna arrived too! Of course. Of course. Don't you worry. Olimp, he begs you not to tell a soul.

OLIMP. Well, if Zarkhin himself knows about it, then it must be true.

(Both leave)

SCENE FIFTEEN

(Enter Ivan)

IVAN. What a shame that I never finished college or anything. It would come in handy in a conversation with a man like Olimp Valerianovich. I think someone is coming.

SCENE SIXTEEN

(Enter Nastya)

IVAN. What splendid scenery.

NASTYA. What happened to my dress?

IVAN. A nymph draped in nothing but a sheet. I wonder what I should do?

NASTYA. Ah! Don't look at me!

IVAN. Mademoiselle, don't think I'm insolent because you are undressed.

NASTYA. Well, I'll be. I thought there was a man in here, but it turns out it's just you, Ivan Ivanovich.

IVAN. Anastasiya Nikolayevna! What are you doing here?

NASTYA. Incidentally, I don't even know where I am.

IVAN. How is it you don't know where you are, Anastasiya Nikolayevna, when you're wandering around naked like you own the place?

NASTYA. Ivan Ivanovich, it's not my fault that my dress was sunk.

IVAN. What do you mean, your dress was sunk?

NASTYA. Naturally, I don't expect you to believe it, but I stand before you a drowned woman.

IVAN. Drowned? Where did you drown?

NASTYA. On a chair.

IVAN. If you take me for a total fool, Anastasiya Nikolayevna, you'll never be able to convince me of it.

NASTYA. Ivan Ivanovich, one might say I'm a walking disaster zone, and meanwhile, you do nothing but doubt.

IVAN. Pardon me, Anastasiya Nikolayevna, but how did you get here?

NASTYA. How? Partly by cab and partly by hand.

IVAN. By hand? What are you, Anastasiya Nikolayevna? An actress? Only actors walk on their hands.

NASTYA. First of all, actresses walk on their own hands. I came here on somebody else's hands.

IVAN. Somebody else's?

NASTYA. That's right.

IVAN. Through the streets?

NASTYA. That's right.

IVAN. Draped in a sheet?

NASTYA. What, do you think I'm a cheap woman or something?

IVAN. What were you in then?

NASTYA. A trunk.

IVAN. I don't get it, Anastasiya Nikolayevna. You'd better explain every-thing to me from the beginning.

NASTYA. All right, Ivan Ivanovich. Let's take it from the beginning. First they dressed me in a gorgeous dress. Then they drenched me with water.

Then they stuffed me in a trunk and brought me here.

IVAN. I don't get it. And what did they do with you when you got here?

NASTYA. They undressed me and took me to bed.

IVAN. Now I get it, Anastasiya Nikolayevna. You've gone down the road to ruin.

NASTYA. You don't say!

IVAN. As God is my witness.

NASTYA. Listen, that's not very nice.

IVAN. Anastasiya Nikolayevna, you should know that your Nadezhda Petrovna is a trader in live goods.

NASTYA. You'll never make me believe even that.

IVAN. Then why do you think she would take chaste maidens, pack them in trunks and send them off to strange men?

NASTYA. What are they going to do with me, Ivan Ivanovich?

IVAN. I think Olimp Valerianovich wants to make you his favorite.

NASTYA. His what?

IVAN. His favorite, Anastasiya Nikolayevna. In other words, a cook of earthly delights.

NASTYA. Oh, mama! They want to drive an unmarried woman into shame. Wait a minute, Ivan Ivanovich. Maybe it's like in "The Bloody Martyr Queen"?

IVAN. What happens in "The Bloody Martyr Queen"?

NASTYA. That's a story about how a cultured milord abducts a nondescript mademoiselle from the lower classes and marries her in a Catholic Church for reasons of passionate love.

IVAN. Anastasiya Nikolayevna, there is no such thing as love in the Soviet state. The only thing we have left is the problem of sex. And furthermore, why should a man like Olimp Valerianovich want to marry you when he's got so much money he doesn't know what to do with it all? I really turned out to be a fool. I thought I'd come to Olimp Valerianovich and denounce Pavel Sergeyevich as a parasitic element. But it turns out they're all birds of a feather.

NASTYA. Ivan Ivanovich, what do I do now?

IVAN. What can we do, Anastasiya Nikolayevna?! You are a fallen woman.

NASTYA. Ivan Ivanovich, you're an educated man. Do something!

(Ivan kneels and kisses Nastya's hand)

IVAN. I bow not before you, but before your suffering. Farewell, Anastasiya Nikolayevna, I must leave you.

NASTYA. Ivan Ivanovich, let me go with you!

IVAN. Where can you go looking like that, Anastasiya Nikolayevna? Any citizen might lodge a complaint with any policeman that you are trying to turn the public streets into a private bathhouse.

NASTYA. Ivan Ivanovich reject not my prayers! Stay with me! Defend me!

IVAN. Here? Come now, Anastasiya Nikolayevna. If Olimp Valerianovich were to find us here in such intimate circumstances, you can forget elevators. He'd throw me down the stairs. Wait! Shh! Somebody's coming. Hide me, Anastasiya Nikolayevna! Hide me! Otherwise, it's down the stairs for sure.

NASTYA. Defend me, Ivan Ivanovich! Defend me!

IVAN. Crawl back here! Crawl back here! *(He sets up a screen)*

(Nastya and Ivan hide behind it)

For God's sake, at least cover my head with your sheet, otherwise they might find me!

SCENE SEVENTEEN

(Enter Olimp, Valerian and Avtonom)

OLIMP. Are you sure the dress is dry?

AVTONOM. It's dry, Olimp. It's dry.

NASTYA. Don't come back here, please. There's a naked woman here.

OLIMP. Pardon me. I see it pleased you to rise, Your Highness. Shall you command us to dress you, Your Highness?

IVAN. What did I tell you? He's made you his favorite.

NASTYA. Now the problems begin.

AVTONOM. Would you care to bathe yourself, Your Highness? Here's a wash tub.

IVAN. A wash tub? Aha. Just as I figured.

NASTYA. You can kill me if you want, but I will not be dishonored.

OLIMP. Forgive me, Your Highness. If you misunderstood me, Your Highness, then please believe me, it was unintended, Your Highness.

NASTYA. You can't fool me with intonations like that. I won't stay here for anything.

OLIMP. But, Your Highness, how could you doubt the passionate loyalty and love of a true Russian?

NASTYA. Love? You're teasing.

OLIMP. I swear it, Your Highness.

AVTONOM. Stay with us, Your Highness.

NASTYA. But what if someone finds out the situation I'm in here? No, I'd better leave.

OLIMP. We implore you, Your Highness. Stay with us. We'll give you a new name. I'll take it all on myself, Your Highness.

NASTYA. Are you blowing hot air or is that the truth?

VALERIAN. As God is our witness, Your Highness.

NATYA. What did I tell you, Ivan Ivanovich. Just like in "The Bloody Martyr Queen." My dear boy, I accept. Only why do you keep calling me "Your Highness"?

VALERIAN. Have no fear, Your Highness. No one will hear us.

NASTYA. But when we get married, will you call me Nastya?

VALERIAN. What do you mean, when we get married?

OLIMP. Avtonom. Water. I need a glass of water!

IVAN. You hear that? He's backing down.

VALERIAN. Papa, I think I'm going to be sick.

IVAN. You hear that? He's backing down.

NASTYA. Listen here, you are terribly heartless. Why did you just declare your love and offer to give me a new name?

AVTONOM. Answer her, Valerian! Answer her!

VALERIAN. Uncle, I can't. My head is spinning. I've got the hiccups.

AVTONOM. Olimp, what's wrong with you?

OLIMP. Just a second. Your Highness, could he possibly dream of such happiness?

NASTYA. You mean he's agreed?

IVAN. Help! My pot is busted.

OLIMP. What's that, Your Highness?

NASTYA. It's nothing. I was just talking to myself. And if you think that my voice has changed, that's only because I caught a cold.

AVTONOM. What is wrong with you, Olimp? Ask her! Ask her!

VALERIAN. Papa, ask her!

OLIMP. When would it suit you, Your Highness?

NASTYA. When would what suit me?

OLIMP. In the event that you've forgotten, Your Highness, I have in mind the wedding ceremony.

NASTYA. Oh, that. Right away.

IVAN. They'll deceive you, Anastasiya Nikolayevna. I'm telling you they'll deceive you. And, anyway, how am I going to get out of here? How am I going to get out of here?

VALERIAN. Papa, look at her leg.

OLIMP. I see, Valerian. You can tell in an instant she's from the nobility.

NASTYA. Listen, close your eyes for just a minute. I'd like to go into the next room.

AVTONOM. Close your eyes, gentlemen! Close your eyes!

OLIMP. Our eyes are closed, Your Highness.

NASTYA. Now get out of here, Ivan Ivanovich. Only do it quietly. Like this. On tiptoe.

IVAN. I'm sunk.

NASTYA. What?

IVAN. I'm sunk, Anastasiya Nikolayevna. I hear somebody coming.

NASTYA. That was just me sniffling, gentlemen. Don't pay it any mind. *(To Ivan)* Hide somewhere. Anywhere. I'll get you out later.

SCENE EIGHTEEN

(The same, minus Ivan)

NASTYA. Hand me my toilet, please.

OLIMP. Certainly, Your Highness.

NASTYA. I'll be ready shortly. *(Leaves)*

SCENE NINETEEN

(Enter Anatoly at a run)

ANATOLY. Papa, the carriage has arrived.

AVTONOM. Anatoly, shut your eyes.

OLIMP. What carriage?

ANATOLY. The wedding carriage. For Valerian and Varvara Sergeyevna.

OLIMP. What Varvara Sergeyevna?

AVTONOM. Oh my God. They'll be here soon.

OLIMP. I forgot. I totally forgot. What are we going to do, Valerian?

VALERIAN. I don't know, papa. My head is spinning.

OLIMP. Avtonom, is that you?

ANATOLY. It's me, papa. It's not him, it's me. Me.

OLIMP. Oh, it's you? Then where are you, Avtonom?

AVTONOM. Here he is.

OLIMP. Avtonom, won't you please go inform them as diplomatically as possible that the wedding is off?

AVTONOM. Diplomatically? I'll try, Olimp. I'll try. But, just think, Olimp. Can you believe what has happened? At the present moment, this woman stands as the last representative of all Russia. And he is going to marry her.

OLIMP. That's right, Avtonom. One might even say he has become the bridegroom of all Russia. What a responsibility.

AVTONOM. And what a dowry.

VALERIAN. Ah!

AVTONOM. Pardon me, Anatoly.

VALERIAN. That's strange, uncle. You boxed my ear but you beg Anatoly's pardon.

SCENE TWENTY

(Enter Nastya)

NASTYA. Here I am, gentlemen. Dressed and hoofed.
OLIMP. Your Highness, the carriage is ready.
NASTYA. Shall we go, then?

(Nastya, Olimp and Valerian leave)

SCENE TWENTY-ONE

AVTONOM. So, Anatoly. You will soon be the brother of the Empress, her
  Highness.
ANATOLY. If only mama were still alive, uncle, wouldn't she be happy?

SCENE TWENTY-TWO

(Enter Agafangel with glue)

AGAFANGEL. Here is your glue, your excellency.
AVTONOM. Glue? What glue? Oh, yes. Anatoly.
ANATOLY. Yes, uncle.
AVTONOM. Right now, you and I are going to glue this picture to a piece of
  cardboard.
ANATOLY. Uncle, is that the uncle of the woman who was in the trunk?
AVTONOM. Yes, Anatoly. The Sovereign of Russia.
ANATOLY. What do we need him for now?
AGAFANGEL. To take with morning coffee, Anatoly Olimpovich.
AVTONOM. To take with coffee?! To embolden our spirits! What are a
  people without a tsar? Orphans, that's what. Everything in nature has a
  tsar. Take a bird, for example. Say, a sparrow or a duck. Even they have a
  tsar. Anatoly.
ANATOLY. Yes, uncle.
AVTONOM. Who is the tsar of the birds?
ANATOLY. The eagle, uncle.
AVTONOM. Agafangel.
AGAFANGEL. Yes, your excellency.
AVTONOM. Who is the tsar of the beasts?
AGAFANGEL. The pig, your excellency.
AVTONOM. The pig? What pig? Why the pig?
AGAFANGEL. Because a pig is tough, your excellency.

AVTONOM. What is so tough about a pig?

AGAFANGEL. Pig's feet, your excellency.

ANATOLY. Uncle, I've already smeared the Grand Duke. What do you want me to stick him on?

AVTONOM. Agafangel, go find some cardboard. And don't forget to peek into the bathroom and see whether anyone else is in there. Otherwise, the Grand Duchess might happen upon another of her close relatives.

(Agafangel leaves)

SCENE TWENTY-THREE

ANATOLY. Where should I put it, uncle?

AVTONOM. Set in on the chair for now.

(Anatoly sets the portrait of the Tsar on the chair, glued side up)

SCENE TWENTY-FOUR

(Enter Nadezhda, Varvara in a wedding dress and Pavel with a portrait)

NADEZHDA. Thank God, we've finally arrived, Avtonom Sigismundovich.

AVTONOM. Oh, what a spot! How am I going to say this diplomatically?

NADEZHDA. These, Avtonom Sigismundovich, are my children.

AVTONOM. I sympathize with you terribly, Nadezhda Petrovna. But, as God is my witness, it isn't my fault.

NADEZHDA. Pardon me?

AVTONOM. How am I going to tell them?

NADEZHDA. Where is the groom, Avtonom Sigismundovich?

VARVARA. Mama, don't say things like that. I get embarrassed.

AVTONOM. I wholeheartedly concur, mademoiselle. It's best not to talk about it.

ANATOLY. If you mean my brother, he left with my papa to get married.

NADEZHDA. Saints alive! Here we stand talking nonsense and they're waiting for us at the church! Pavel, powder Varvara's nose. Let's go, Avtonom Sigismundovich! Let's go!

AVTONOM. The thing is, Nadezhda Petrovna, I've got to tell you...

NADEZHDA. Oh, my goodness! I forgot. Just a minute, Avtonom Sigismundovich. Varya, get down on your knees.

VARVARA. But we...

NADEZHDA. Varya, don't hold things up. Avtonom Sigismundovich, we'll be ready in just a moment.

(Varvara kneels. Nadezhda begins weeping and wailing. Pavel powders Varvara's nose)

VARVARA. Mama, please don't drip on my dress. Cry over there, mama. Drip on the floor.

AVTONOM. What is wrong, Nadezhda Petrovna?

NADEZHDA. Oh, I'm giving you and your mother away to a stranger's father! But a stranger can never be a father to you. And a stranger can never be a mother to you. Oh, fathers! Oh, mothers! *(She weeps and wails)*

AVTONOM. Nadezhda Petrovna, I am very pleased that things have taken such a turn. There's no need to suffer so, Nadezhda Petrovna. The wedding is off.

THE THREE GULYACHKINS. What do you mean?

AVTONOM. Don't worry, Nadezhda Petrovna, there will be no wedding.

VARVARA. Mama, I think I've just been humiliated.

NADEZHDA. What do you mean, there will be no wedding? Why not?

AVTONOM. I'm afraid I can't tell you that.

NADEZHDA. Saints alive, what is going on? They've humiliated us, that's what they've done. They've humiliated us. Mister Avtonom Sigismundovich, what have we done to displease Valerian Olimpovich? It would seem that my daughter is perfectly plump and is incapable of being humiliated. If he thinks that Varya's nose isn't very successful, he should know that even without her nose she'll make a very pleasant spouse.

VARVARA. In fact, Avtonom Sigismundovich, if you look at it from a different point of view, you'll see that it is quite prominent. Quite prominent, really.

ANATOLY. I think I can see that.

AVTONOM. The problem is not in her nose, Nadezhda Petrovna, it's much deeper.

VARVARA. Deeper? Avtonom Sigismundovich, even deeper I have....

AVTONOM. I believe you. I believe you. But, please understand, Varvara Sergeyevna, you are not the problem.

NADEZHDA. Then who is, Avtonom Sigismundovich? Who is? If I am the problem, Avtonom Sigismundovich, you should know that I am just her mother. Nothing but rubbish and nonsense, Avtonom Sigismundovich.

AVTONOM. I agree with you wholeheartedly, Nadezhda Petrovna, only....

NADEZHDA. Were I in Valerian Olimpovich's place, I wouldn't pay me the slightest attention.

AVTONOM. You are absolutely right, Nadezhda Petrovna. However, the problem lies elsewhere.

NADEZHDA. What is the problem, Avtonom Sigismundovich?

AVTONOM. That, Nadezhda Petrovna, is a secret, and I can't explain it to you.

NADEZHDA. You can't? Pavlusha, you're obstinate. You talk with him, please.

PAVEL. Listen here, young man! Are you trying to drag our family's collective nose through the dirt? Why is the wedding off?

AVTONOM. Don't you dare talk to me like that.

PAVEL. Don't dare? And what if I'm accustomed to having intimate chats with the Third Internationale? What will you do then?

AVTONOM. Now I've had it. Now he's going to arrest me.

PAVEL. I'll have you know that I went underground for the whole October Revolution. And you tell me, "don't dare"!

AVTONOM. He's going to shoot me.

PAVEL. For all you know, I might be a chairman…, of a housing committee. I am an autocrat!

AVTONOM. My apologies, comrade. I didn't….

PAVEL. Silence! I am a party man.

ANATOLY. Shut up! I am the brother of her Highness!

(Pavel sits on the chair)

SCENE TWENTY-FIVE

(Enter Stepan Stepanovich and his wife Felitsiata Gordeyevna carrying flowers)

FELITSIATA GORDEYEVNA. Christ is risen, Avtonom Sigismundovich. Pay no attention to my kisses, because my spirit is as pure as an Easter service.

STEPAN STEPANOVICH. Forgive me for failing to inquire about your health, but one must put the interests of the motherland above all.

SCENE TWENTY-SIX

(Enter Ilinkin and Ilinkina)

ILINKIN. Ladies and gentlemen! Please don't tell me that Mikhail Alexandrovich is a bad joke.

FELITSIATA GORDEYEVNA. Listen here. How can you put such a question so tastelessly?

SCENE TWENTY-SEVEN

(Enter Zotik Frantsevich Zarkhin, Ariadna Pavlinovna Zarkhina and their daughters Tosya and Syusya)

ARIADNA PAVLINOVNA. You can't imagine how self-assured these bolsheviks are. Just now my husband and I were walking along the street and a policeman was standing on the corner pretending that nothing has happened.

SCENE TWENTY-EIGHT

(Enter Narkis Smaragdovich Krantik)

NARKIS SMARAGDOVICH. What do you think, wouldn't an eight-by-twelve be splendid?

ZOTIK FRANTSEVICH. What eight-by-twelve?

NARKIS SMARAGDOVICH. Well, I thought it might be nice to fix this moment for posterity.

STEPAN STEPANOVICH. Fix what?

NARKIS SMARAGDOVICH. The renaissance.

ILINKIN. What renaissance?

NARKIS SMARAGDOVICH. The rebirth. The rebirth of our long-suffering motherland. This event is bound to send shock-waves through all of Russia. As such, I've decided a cabinet picture is the most appropriate. Eight-by-twelve. (Pulls out a large camera)

FELITSIATA GORDEYEVNA. Stepan, it's a photographer.

NARKIS SMARAGDOVICH. Narkis Smaragdovich Krantik at your service. Amateur photographer. Having learned under sworn secret that the empress, her Highness is here….

PAVEL. What highness? Here?

AVTONOM. The cat is out of the bag. Hold him! Hold him! Agafangel!

SCENE TWENTY-NINE

(Enter Agafangel)

AGAFANGEL. Yes, your excellency.

AVTONOM. Cover all the exits!

(Holding a pistol, Agafangel takes a position by the door)

VOICES. What happened? What's going on? What is this?

AVTONOM. Gentlemen, they've been spying on us.

ARIADNA PAVLINOVNA. Who has been spying on us?

AVTONOM. The communists.

ALL. Communists!

FELITSIATA GORDEYEVNA. Every man for himself!

(Everyone races for the door)

AGAFANGEL. Stop or I'll shoot!

STEPAN STEPANOVICH. Help! They've got us surrounded!

NARKIS SMARAGDOVICH. It looks to me like there's only one communist. Let's try surrounding him.

AVTONOM. That's right, gentlemen! Surround him! Surround him!

VARVARA. Mama, if they kill Pavel, it will simply be a nightmare.

ARIADNA PAVLINOVNA. Gentlemen, don't surround him only from behind. Surround him in front, too. No need to fear, Mister Ilinkin. Go ahead, surround him in front.

ALL. Surround him! Surround him!

PAVEL. Mama, I am perishing in the clutches of the bourgeoisie.

NADEZHDA. Good people, don't cause the ruination of a Christian believer. Avtonom Sigismundovich, it's true that if you look at him from one angle he's a communist, but if you look at him from another...

PAVEL. From the other I'm nothing of the sort. (He stands and bows. The portrait of Tsar Nikolai has stuck to his rear end)

ARIADNA PAVLINOVNA. Zotik, don't believe him! Don't believe him, Zotik! Don't go near him!

ZOTIK FRANTSEVICH. But we have got to discern his true face.

TOSYA. Papa, he has two of them.

ZOTIK FRANTSEVICH. What do you mean, two?

TOSYA. Well, papa, I'm a bit ashamed to say it, but he has a face on his rear end.

ALL. Where?

TOSYA. Right here.

AVTONOM. All right, young man. Bend over. Oh my God! Attention!

PAVEL. Mama, whose face am I wearing back there? Mine?

ANATOLY. No. It's ours.

SCENE THIRTY

(Enter Valerian and Guests)

VALERIAN. Gentlemen, prepare yourselves. Her Highness is coming.

ALL. She's coming!

AVTONOM. Gentlemen, she's coming.

ARIADNA PAVLINOVNA. Is she almost here?

VALERIAN. Almost, madame, almost. (Runs out)

SCENE THIRTY-ONE

ILINKIN. Finally! Capital will return to the capitalists.

FELITSIATA GORDEYEVNA. I always told you it couldn't last.

STEPAN STEPANOVICH. Indeed, how could it have gone on when they have utterly destroyed the whole country. Top to bottom. Beginning with our factory and ending with our candy store.

ZOTIK FRANTSEVICH. They called us labor exploiters and they said they supported free labor. I suppose that if free labor means the whole country is out of work, then they were right. Only I can't see what's so good about that.

ILINKINA. Who cares about your candy store when I had all my silver spoons confiscated in nineteen-nineteen?

ARIADNA PAVLINOVNA. Look at what's happened to the schools! They're nothing but a den of thieves. Boys study in one class with girls! Maybe they can study algebra or music together, but what about anatomy class?

AVTONOM. Ariadna Pavlinovna, just imagine what might have happened if in the old days I had studied anatomy with girls.

ILINKINA. Who cares about anatomy when I had all my silver spoons confiscated in nineteen-nineteen?

FELITSIATA GORDEYEVNA. Who cares about school when you can't even go out on the streets anymore? In peacetime there was art everywhere. Take the monument of General Skobelev, for example. You'd look at him and you could just feel what a pleasant sight that was for sore eyes. Now look at the statue they replaced him with. Pardon the expression, but it looks to me like the new guy is making obscene gestures.

ARIADNA PAVLINOVNA. That's just what it is, an obscene gesture. I always go for walks on that square and I know just what you're talking about.

ILINKINA. Who cares about obscene gestures when I had all my silver spoons confiscated in nineteen-nineteen?

ILINKIN. Gentlemen, have you noticed what they have done with religious people? Take me, for example. Every Sunday I get an urge for religion, but they've put kindergartens in all the churches. As a result, you either have to travel all the way across town to get your religion or you have to go without it altogether.

ARIADNA PAVLINOVNA. How can you go without religion? For example, every Sunday I read the Bible to Tosya and Syusya. It is so ennobling, so ennobling. So much so that I don't even recognize my little Tosya any more.

STEPAN STEPANOVICH. Yes, it's terribly difficult with children these days. Tell me, mademoiselle, do you have children?

VARVARA. Oh come now, I would never allow myself something like that.

NADEZHDA. My good man, she is a bride.

STEPAN STEPANOVICH. A bride? There, you see? What has happened to the family these days? Fathers are bachelors, mothers are married and their children are all orphans.

NADEZHDA. You're absolutely right. What a state we are in! In the old days we lived a real life. But what do we have now? A utopia.

FELITSIATA GORDEYEVNA. Well, thank God, the utopia is about to end.

AVTONOM. We put up long enough with the revolution. Now let it put up with us.

SCENE THIRTY-TWO

(Enter Valerian)

GUEST. Ladies and gentleman, they are approaching.

ZOTIK FRANTSEVICH. They're approaching! Stop, gentlemen! Stop!

AVTONOM. Young man, get down on all fours this minute. Face the door. What, are you deaf, young man? I am telling you, face the door. Not with that face, with the other one. Ladies, be so kind. Decorate the portrait with flowers.

(Pavel kneels on all fours with the portrait glued to his rear end. Tosya and Syusya place flowers around the portrait)

ARIADNA PAVLINOVNA. Use white flowers, Tosya, white flowers. And make them forget-me-nots if you can. It will be symbolic.

ILINKIN. Stepan Stepanovich, why did you stand in front of us? My wife is a woman, you know. She can't see over your head.

STEPAN STEPANOVICH. I believe that my services to the fatherland allow me...

ILINKIN. Stepan Stepanovich, what services to the fatherland?

STEPAN STEPANOVICH. My good sir, I am nothing less than an active counterrevolutionary.

ILINKIN. But what have you done, if I may ask?

STEPAN STEPANOVICH. For all you know, I may have called a communist "Mister" instead of "comrade" at a perilous moment. And what have you done?

ILINKINA. Petya, let him stand in front. Who knows, maybe he's telling the truth.

PAVEL. Help! I've been stabbed!

ALL. What happened?

PAVEL. Mama, they're making me into a pin cushion.

NADEZHDA. Ladies, if you can, please try to pin them to his pants and not to his body. If his pants get ruined, it's no great loss.

AGAFANGEL. Your excellency, they are coming.

AVTONOM. As soon as they enter, everyone shout "Hurrah!"

SCENE THIRTY-THREE

(Enter the Hurdy-Gurdy Man, the Drummer and the Woman with a Parrot and Tambourine)

ALL. Hurrah!

AVTONOM. What the hell is this? Who are you?

HURDY-GURDY MAN. We are guests, my good man, guests.

AVTONOM. Whose guests?

DRUMMER. Your guests, my good man, your guests.

HURDY-GURDY MAN. Olimp Valerianovich was kind enough to invite us to the wedding, and so, as you can see, we have arrived.

ANATOLY. They're probably the musicians.

AVTONOM. Say, do you happen to know the kind of music that is played at court?

WOMAN WITH A PARROT AND TAMBOURINE. What a strange question, my good man. We've been playing in courtyards our whole life.

AVTONOM. In that case, stand over here.

TOSYA. Mama, look how pretty the symbol came out.

AGAFANGEL. Your excellency, they are approaching.

AVTONOM. Attention, gentlemen, attention. More gaiety, gentlemen, more gaiety.

VARVARA. Pavlusha, smile!

NADEZHDA. Pavlusha, when she walks past you, don't forget to ask her to give us a grocery store.

PAVEL. Mama, I can't ask from that side. You'd better ask her yourself.

AGAFANGEL. Her Highness, the Empress!

AVTONOM. Present arms! Attention! Music! Play the anthem!

SCENE THIRTY-FOUR

(Enter Nastya, Olimp, Valerian and Father Pavsikakhy)

ALL. Hur-r-r-ah!

PAVEL. Don't hang me, Your Highness. For God's sake, don't hang me!

NADEZHDA. Have mercy on him, Your Highness! He did it out of stupidity. Truly, he did it out of stupidity.

NASTYA. What are you clinging to my hem for? Oh my God, it's the mistress.

76

NADEZHDA. Oh my God, it's Nastya.

ALL. Hur-r-r-ah!

PAVEL. Mama, fan me with something or I'm going to pass away here in front of everyone.

OLIMP. Gentlemen. This day Her Royal Highness has graciously agreed to graciously enter into wedlock with my son Valerian Olimpovich.

VARVARA. Ah!

ALL. Hur-r-r-ah!

OLIMP. Dear ladies and gentlemen! I weep.

VARVARA. I do too.

NADEZHDA. Varya! Shut up!

AVTONOM. Dear ladies and gentlemen! Her Royal Highness thanks you for your hearty welcome. Dear ladies and gentlemen...

OLIMP. Your Royal Highness...

AVTONOM. Olimp, shut up a minute, will you? I'll keep it short.

OLIMP. For seven years I remained silent. I can remain silent no more. Seven years, Your Royal Highness, I have waited seven years for this day and finally it has come.

FATHER PAVSIKAKHY. Dear Christian believers, long shall ye live.

ALL. Long shall we live. Long shall we live.

AVTONOM. What in the world are you playing?

HURDY-GURDY MAN. Sorry about that. The key won't seem to stay in tune.

OLIMP. Your Royal Highness, what is the Russian intelligentsia? The Russian intelligentsia is an angel, an unseen angel soaring high above Russia. Please allow me, Your Royal Highness, to say a few words in the stead of this angel.

NASTYA. Hit it.

OLIMP. Seven years, Your Royal Highness, seven years our heads have been covered in filth. Seven years. And each one of them has seemed like a decade. But what am I saying? What decade? Each one of them has passed as though it were an entire century. Seven hundred years, Your Royal Highness, our heads have been covered with filth.

ALL. Bravo! Bravo!

OLIMP. And even when the white guard mixed the blood of its sons with the priceless blood of our martyred motherland, even then our heads were covered with filth. Even then we were accused of violence, we were accused of being predators, we were accused of executions. But I now stand face to face, eye to eye with the personification of all of Russia. And I say to her, "no." I shout with all my might, "Show us that man whom we executed! Let him come forth and accuse us. But he will never come forth, because he is not here."

ALL. Bravo! Bravo!

OLIMP. Your Royal Highness, I bare before you my heart and I stand before you as naked as the day I was born.

SYUSYA. Papa! Bend over, I want to see!

OLIMP. And I say to you, "Yes." Yes, Your Royal Highness. Yes, we loved our people. Oh, Your Royal Highness, oh, how we loved our people! I, for example, devoted my entire life to the working people. I had a factory and there were five-hundred people working in it. And I loved those people. But they were taken away from me and I am prepared to die getting them back, because without those people I can't live. Your Royal Highness, give us back our people.

ALL. Give us back our people!

OLIMP. Yes, Your Royal Highness, we loved our people and we loved our land. But are they capable of loving? How could they love their people and their land when they have never owned either people or land? But I, Your Royal Highness, owned land. Lots of land. Almost a thousand acres of nothing but land. And they took it away from me. They deprived me of my wet-nurse, my mother and my mama.

ZOTIK FRANTSEVICH. Your Royal Highness, give us back our mama!

OLIMP. But most of all we loved Russia. And what do we see now? She is gone. They replaced her. They pulled her out from under our feet. And now we hang suspended in the air, Your Highness. I hang in the air as if I were weightless. Yes, Your Highness, we have been deprived of weight and we hang in the air, while beneath us there is no Russia to be seen for thousands and thousands of miles. What will we do if we suddenly plunge back to earth, Your Highness? There is nowhere for us to fall. But I believed, I always believed, Your Highness, that a new Columbus would appear and discover Russia. He has appeared, this Columbus, and this Columbus is you. The waves are still stormy, but our course is right. We have already heard the joyous cry of "land!" ring out from the mast. A thousand acres of it. My land.

FATHER PAVSIKAKHY. Dear Christian believers, save our native land!

ALL. We'll save our land! We'll save it!

AVTONOM. Music! Fanfare! Hurrah!

ALL. Hur-r-r-ah!

NASTYA. Wow! What a wedding!

ALL. Hur-r-r-ah!

(When the cheer dies down, a long shriek is heard)

VOICES. Did you hear that? What was that? What was that?

NASTYA. Oh my God, that was probably Ivan Ivanovich screaming in terror in the next room.

OLIMP. Gentlemen, perhaps the people are already celebrating.

ARIADNA PAVLINOVNA. Do you think they already know?

OLIMP. Of course they know. Why else would they start shouting "hurrah"?

ZOTIK FRANTSEVICH. Are you sure they were shouting "hurrah"?

OLIMP. I heard it as plain as day.

STEPAN STEPANOVICH. Then the people are with us! Hurrah!

ALL. Hur-r-ah!

OLIMP. Listen.

VOICE OF IVAN. Help!

ZOTIK FRANTSEVICH. Did you hear anything?

AVTONOM. No. Did you?

ZOTIK FRANTSEVICH. Me either.

STEPAN STEPANOVICH. Let's try again.

ALL. Hur-r-r-r-a-a-h!

OLIMP. Listen.

AVTONOM. The people are silent.

NASTYA. God help us if they ever try to have their say again.

PAVEL. Women, men and even children! Take note of the terrible hero standing before you!

VOICES. What happened? What was that? What's going on?

PAVEL. Women, men and even children! This dame has her sights set on the throne. But she will mount it only over my dead body. That is my absolutely official declaration to you.

VOICES. What is he saying? Is he insane? Your Highness, he's insane.

PAVEL. Comrades. What did we, workers of the plough, and chairmen of housing committees, struggle for? Why did we fall as victims on the blood-red battlefields? Women, men and even children, I refuse, I categorically and heroically refuse to swear loyalty to the social order of generals, priests and petty bourgeoisie.

VOICES. Don't let him speak! Make him shut up!

PAVEL. Comrades. No one can make us remain silent about this. Forever, we will speak in unison about generals, priests and the petty bourgeoisie because this is our idea. It is our holy obsession. Women, men and even children, you will not be able to strangle the revolution as long as we are here…, that is, me and my mama. And don't you think that it's only her that I'm not afraid of. Nothing of the sort. I can go to England and I won't even fear the English Queen. I'll tell off any tsar there is. And don't think that kings will avoid my wrath just because they are far away. Comrades, I am a man of enormous scope. This very instant, in fact, I declare before all tsars, be they English, Italian, Turkish or French, "Tsars!…," mama, what's going to happen next?!… "Tsars!… You're all… rapscallions!"

AVTONOM. Gentlemen, it's a plot. Arrest him immediately.

VOICES. Arrest him! Arrest him!

NASTYA. Leave him alone. He's drunk.

AVTONOM. Your word is law for me, Your Highness, but…

PAVEL. Drunk? Who's drunk? I'm drunk? I could breathe in any man's face right now and he wouldn't smell a thing. That is the whole point, comrades, I am dead sober. The point is that I am capable of this even when sober. And I demand that you fix for posterity the words I am about to say, because, for having said them, I may be in for a promotion. Your Imperial Highness, you… are a bitch.

ALL. A-h-h!

NASTYA. The same goes for you.

AVTONOM. Guards!

AGAFANGEL. Yes, your excellency.

AVTONOM. Seize him!

VOICES. Seize him! Tie him up!

PAVEL. Comrades! She's a cook. As God is my witness, a cook!

NADEZHDA. Good sirs, she is a cook. Honest. A cook.

VARVARA. It's Nastya the cook.

THE THREE GULYACHKINS. A cook!

AVTONOM. What?

PAVEL. Respected comrades, she is our cook.

AVTONOM. Silence!

PAVEL. Honest, she's a cook. She used to wash my socks and fry meatballs. I'm telling the truth.

OLIMP. There is no doubt about it. He's insane.

NADEZHDA. My dear people, it's God's truth. She fries our meatballs. Nastya, you slut, answer your mistress. Do you fry our meatballs or not?

NASTYA. Doubtlessly.

NADEZHDA. Did you hear that, good people? She admitted it. She admitted it as if on God's tribunal.

OLIMP. Your Highness…

NADEZHDA. Who's Highness is she? Her name is Pupkina. I even have her papers with me. Pupkina. Anastasiya Nikolayevna Pupkina.

OLIMP. Pupkina?

NADEZHDA. Pupkina. From the town of Povetkino in the province of Tula.

OLIMP. Your Imperial Highness, what does this mean, "Pupkina"?

NASTYA. Nothing in particular.

VALERIAN. Pupkina?

NASTYA. Pupkina.

OLIMP. And your uncle?

NASTYA. What about him?

OLIMP. Do you have an uncle?

NASTYA. Yes.

OLIMP. A duke?

NASTYA. What do you think, we're foreigners or something?

OLIMP. Who is he then?

NASTYA. A sexton.

OLIMP. Hold on to me! Hold me! Gentlemen, I think I'm going to rise up into the air again.

ZOTIK FRANTSEVICH. That's it. All is lost.

NARKIS SMARAGDOVICH. The renaissance is over.

OLIMP. You mean, once again, nothing exists? Neither she, nor I, nor you?

PAVEL. Comrades. You're right about that. There's nothing anywhere. But my words live on. My heroism, comrades, remains. No one can ever deny the fact that I called the heiress to the Russian throne a bitch. Do you realize what my potential is? For having said something like that they might start letting me enter the Kremlin without a pass. They might build a sanatorium in the name of Pavel Gulyachkin. Comrades, do you really think that just because they took away my grocery store and tore down the sign on it that they destroyed me along with them? No comrades. I'm willing to hang out a new sign and I'll bargain under it with everything of value in the world. I'll sell anything, I don't care what it is.

VOICES. Comrade Gulyachkin, don't ruin us! He's the one to blame. He's the one.

PAVEL. Aha, my little dears! So you're scared are you? You think that if you go turning my rear end into a mini picture gallery that I'm going to thank you for it, do you? You think you can turn a man's face inside out and that I'm going to remain silent about it? No, my dears. No. I'll destroy all of you. All of you!

VOICES. Don't ruin us! Have mercy! We don't want to die for nothing!

PAVEL. Silence! Do you know what I'm capable of? When I get an idea in my head, I'm capable of anything. For the sake of an idea, I made myself into a dowry. And now I'll marry Varya off to all of Russia! Varya! Pick any one you want.

NADEZHDA. Go on, Varya. Pick somebody.

VOICES. Me! Choose me! Over here!

VARVARA. I want a passionate man in a pince-nez.

FELITSIATA GORDEYEVNA. My husband! Choose my husband!

TOSYA. Choose my papa!

OLIMP. Ladies and gentlemen, what is going on here? I saw it all with my own eyes. Right here on this very spot. Our passionately beloved motherland, our rough-hewn Mother Russia rose like a Phoenix from a trunk.

STEPAN STEPANOVICH. What trunk?

OLIMP. Avtonom. Anatoly. Bring in the trunk.

(They carry in the trunk)

Ladies and gentlemen, I was standing right here.

AVTONOM. And I was right here.

VALERIAN. And I was over here, holding a muffin.

ANATOLY. And I was by the cactus.

AVTONOM. And I opened the lock.

OLIMP. And Russia rose before us.

IVAN. (*Appears out of the trunk with with the pot on his head*) I heard and saw everything.

(*All shriek and scatter*)

Comrades. Keep your wits about you and don't go far because all of you are going to be hung.

VOICES. Save us, Pavel Sergeyevich! Save us, Pavel Sergeyevich! Tell him, Pavel Sergeyevich! Pavel Sergeyevich!

IVAN. Police! Police! Police!

OLIMP. Excuse me, comrade. What do the police have to do with this?

IVAN. I'm going to report you.

OLIMP. What are you going to report?

IVAN. That right here in your own apartment, right here in this dining room, you have overthrown the Soviet government.

NASTYA. Vanya, quit your blathering.

OLIMP. Comrade, it just seemed that way, honest. It's not true. We have witnesses. Here's a communist, for instance.

IVAN. Where's there a communist?

OLIMP. Right here, Pavel Sergeyevich.

IVAN. Pavel Sergeyevich? I'll have you know, citizens, that Pavel Sergeyevich is a False Dmitry and an imposter. He's no communist.

PAVEL. Who's a False Dmitry? I'm a False Dmitry? Me? Comrades! I am a people's tribune. I have callouses. Look at the callouses on my hands. But that's not all. You should see the callouses I have on my feet!

IVAN. You're lying!

PAVEL. I'll prove it.

IVAN. How?

PAVEL. You just call Chicherin[2] in here and ask him whether I'm a communist or not, comrades.

AVTONOM. You're taking a big risk, citizen. He has a warrant.

IVAN. Where's his warrant?

PAVEL. Right here. (*Removes it from his briefcase*)

IVAN. (*Grabs the piece of paper*) You've all had it now, citizens.

---

[2] Georgy Chicherin was a prominent figure in the Communist Party and the People's Commissar of Foreign Affairs.

PAVEL. Grab him! Grab him! Where are you going? Where are you going?

IVAN. To the police, citizens, to the police. *(Runs out)*

PAVEL. Help! Help!

ALL. Help! Help!

PAVEL. I'm done for. They'll hang me, hang me for certain.

OLIMP. What would they hang you for? Can a person like you really be hung, comrade?

PAVEL. True Christian believers, I composed that warrant myself.

VARVARA. Give my regards to mama. I'm dying.

OLIMP. Yourself? What do you mean, yourself? But you're a communist, aren't you?

PAVEL. No, comrades. I'm basically…

OLIMP. Basically what?

PAVEL. Basically, I'm a man of many profiles.

OLIMP. It's over. All is lost. There are no real people. She's not real and he's not real. Maybe we're not real, either?

AVTONOM. Unreal people is one thing, but what do you do when warrants are phony?

ARIADNA PAVLINOVNA. Comrades, I can't be arrested. I have children. See? My little bunnies Tosya and Syusya.

FATHER PAVSIKAKHY. I'm the next best thing to a party member because Jesus Christ was a communist.

PAVEL. Mama, tell them I'm a fool. Tell them I'm stupid. Maybe they don't hang idiots, mama.

NADEZHDA. They won't believe me, Pavlusha. They won't believe me.

PAVEL. Oh yes they will, mama. As God is my witness, they will.

VOICES. They're coming! Oh Lord! Oh my God! We're ruined! We're done for!

OLIMP. Sisters and brothers, we shall suffer for the truth.

VALERIAN. Papa, I think I'm going to be sick.

OLIMP. Just like the first Christians.

(Pause)

SCENE THIRTY-FIVE

(Enter Ivan. He sits on a chair and weeps)

OLIMP. What's wrong? What happened?

IVAN. They refused.

OLIMP. Refused what?

IVAN. They refused to arrest you.

(Pause)

PAVEL. Mama, if they don't even want to arrest us, how are we going to live? Mama, how are we going to live?

THE END

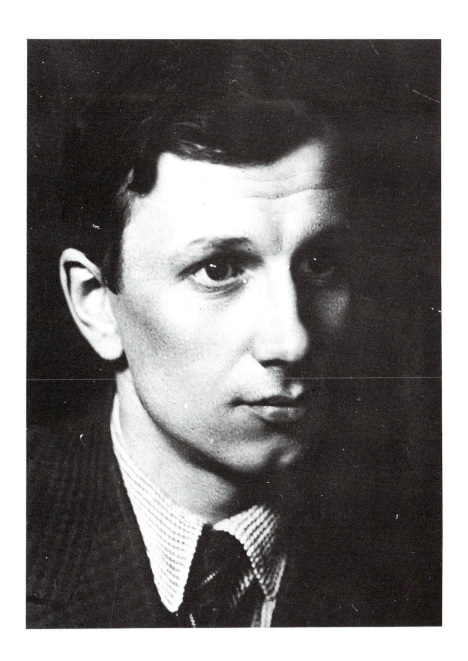

1. Nikolai Erdman, mid-1920s.

2. Vsevolod Meyerhold, Nikolai Erdman, Vladimir Mayakovsky, 1928–9.

3. Vsevolod Meyerhold, Vladimir Mayakovsky, Nikolai Erdman, 1928–9.

4. Nikolai Erdman and the actor Boris Chirkov, 1940s.

5. Nikolai Erdman (third from right) at the funeral of Sergei Yesenin, December 1925. On the left, Vsevolod Meyerhold and his wife, the actress Zinaida Raikh, who was formerly married to Yesenin.

6. Nikolai Erdman with his father Robert Erdman, 1946.

7. Nikolai Erdman, 1950(?).

8. Nikolai Erdman (right) and director Konstantin Yudin (centre) with an unknown stable hand during the filming of *Courageous People*, 1950.

9. Official portrait of Nikolai Erdman, 1951, taken in connection with his receiving the Stalin Prize with Mikhail Volpin for their script to the film *Courageous People*.

10. Nikolai Erdman, early 1960s.

11. Nikolai Erdman, 1965.

12. A scene from *The Warrant* at the Renaissance Theater, Berlin, 1927. Photo: Harvard College Library.

13. A scene from *The Suicide* at the Trinity Square Repertory, Providence, R.I., 1980. Photo: Constance Brown.

14. Derek Meader (Viktor, above) and Richard Jenkins (Semyon, below) in
The Suicide at the Trinity Square Repertory, Providence, R.I., 1980.
Photo: Constance Brown.

15. Veniamin Smekhov (Aristarkh)
and Filipp Antipov (Semyon) in
The Suicide at the Taganka
Theater, Moscow, 1991.

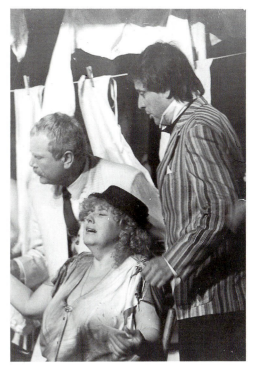

16. Yury Smirnov
(Kalabushkin), Mariya
Politseimako (Mariya)
and Veniamin
Smekhov (Aristarkh)
at the Taganka
Theater, Moscow 1991.

THE SUICIDE

Characters

Semyón Semyónovich Podsekálnikov (also called Sénya)
Maríya Lukyánovna Podsekálnikova, his wife (also called Másha)
Serafíma Ilínishna, his mother-in-law
Alexánder Petróvich Kalábushkin, their neighbor
Margaríta Ivánovna Peresvétova
Stepán Vasílyevich Peresvétov
Aristárkh Dominíkovich Grand-Skúbik
Yegór Timoféyevich (also called Yegórushka)
Nikífor Arséntyevich Pugachyóv, a butcher
Víktor Víktorovich, a writer
Father Yelpídy, a priest
Cleopátra Maxímovna (also called Cápochka)
Raísa Filíppovna
An old lady
Olég Leonídovich
A young deaf-mute boy
Zínka Padespán
Grúnya
A gypsy choir
Kostya, a waiter
A second waiter
A Hatmaker
A Seamstress
Two suspicious types
Two boys
Three men
A church choir
Torchbearers
A deacon
Two old women

ACT I

(A room in Semyon's apartment. Night)

SCENE ONE

(The husband and wife Semyon and Mariya are asleep on a double bed)

SEMYON. Masha, hey Masha! Masha, are you asleep, Masha?

MARIYA. *(Cries out)* A-a-ah...

SEMYON. What's the matter? What's the matter? It's me.

MARIYA. What do you want, Semyon?

SEMYON. Masha, I just wanted to ask... Masha, hey Masha... Are you sleeping again? Masha!

MARIYA. *(Cries out)* A-a-ah...

SEMYON. What's the matter? What's the matter? It's me.

MARIYA. Is that you, Semyon?

SEMYON. Uh-huh, it's me.

MARIYA. What do you want, Semyon?

SEMYON. Masha, I just wanted to ask...

MARIYA. Uh-huh. Well, what is it you want, Semyon? Senya....

SEMYON. Masha, I just wanted to ask... Do we have any liverwurst sausage left over from dinner?

MARIYA. What?

SEMYON. I said, do we have any liverwurst sausage left over from dinner?

MARIYA. Well, Semyon, I might have expected anything from you. But a midnight conversation with an exhausted woman about liverwurst sausage—well that I didn't expect. That is so inconsiderate. So inconsiderate. I work days on end like a horse of some kind, or an ant, and instead of giving me a moment's peace at night, you make my life a bundle of nerves! You know, Semyon, you and your liverwurst sausage have simply destroyed me, destroyed me... Can't you understand, Senya? If you can't sleep yourself, at least let someone else get their sleep. Senya, who do you think I'm talking to? Semyon, are you sleeping? Senya!

SEMYON. A-a-ah...

MARIYA. What's the matter? What's the matter? It's me.

SEMYON. Is that you, Masha?

MARIYA. Uh-huh, it's me.

SEMYON. What do you want, Masha?

MARIYA. I said if you can't sleep, then at least let someone else get their

89

sleep.

SEMYON. Wait a minute, Masha.

MARIYA. No, you wait a minute. Why didn't you eat when you had the chance? If I'm not mistaken, mama and I prepare everything specially for you, just the way you like it. If I'm not mistaken, mama and I serve you more than anybody else.

SEMYON. And why do you and your mama serve me more than anybody else? You don't do that for nothing. You dish up psychology with every meal you serve. You want to prove to everybody that Semyon Semyon-ovich, here, doesn't have a job anywhere, but we serve him more than anybody else. I know why you serve me more than anybody else. You serve me more than anybody else to humiliate me. You...

MARIYA. Wait a minute, Senya.

SEMYON. No, you wait a minute. Because when I lie here starving to death all night long with you in the conjugal bed without any witnesses, tête-à-tête under the same blanket, you start economizing on liverwurst with me.

MARIYA. You think I'm economizing, Senya? Sweetheart, eat all you want. I'll bring you something right now. (*Slides off the bed. Lights a candle and walks to the door*) Lord above, what is happening to us? Huh? It's terribly sad to live like this. (*Goes into the other room*)

SCENE TWO

(*Darkness. Semyon lies silently on the double bed*)

SCENE THREE

(*Mariya returns holding a candle in one hand and a plate with some bread and liverwurst in the other*)

MARIYA. How do you want your liverwurst spread, Senya, on white or black bread?

SEMYON. The color bears no importance for me because I refuse to eat.

MARIYA. What do you mean you won't eat?

SEMYON. Even if this liverwurst sausage proves to be the death of me, I still refuse to eat it.

MARIYA. What for?

SEMYON. Because I know how you want to spread it. You want to spread it with an introductory speech. First you'll defile my very soul, and only then you'll start spreading your liverwurst.

MARIYA. Listen here, Semyon...

SEMYON. Yeah, I hear you. Get into bed.

MARIYA. What?

SEMYON. Get into bed, I tell you.

MARIYA. First I'll spread the liverwurst and then I'll get into bed.

SEMYON. No you won't.

MARIYA. Yes I will.

SEMYON. Dammit, which one of us is the husband, you or me? Do you think you can control my every move just because I've got no income? You'd be better off thinking about how this life is driving me crazy, Mariya. Just look what you've driven me to. (Sits up in bed and throws off the blanket. He crosses his legs, strikes himself below the knee with the edge of his hand and kicks his leg up in the air) Did you see that?

MARIYA. What was that, Senya?

SEMYON. A nervous symptom.

MARIYA. We can't go on living like this, Semyon. Clowns can do tricks like that in the circus, but a human being can't live like this.

SEMYON. Why not? You think I'm supposed to croak or something? Kick off? Huh? Tell me straight, Mariya, what are you trying to prove? Are you trying to prove that you can deprive me of my last breath? You'll prove it. Only I'll tell you right here in our own little happy family circle, Mariya, you're a real scum.

MARIYA. What?

SEMYON. You're a scum! A bitch! A devil!

(The candle-holder drops out of Mariya's hand, falls on the floor and breaks. The room is totally dark again. Pause)

SCENE FOUR

(Serafima enters the darkened room)

MARIYA. (Cries) A-a-ah…

SERAFIMA. What's the matter? What's the matter? It's me.

MARIYA. Is that you, mama?

SERAFIMA. Uh-huh, it's me.

MARIYA. What do you want, mama?

SERAFIMA. Masha, would you please tell me why things are falling around here in the middle of the night? Huh? You'll wake up everyone in the building. Masha! Hey, Masha! Masha, are you crying? Semyon Semyonovich, what's going on here? Semyon Semyonovich! Masha! I'm asking you, Masha. Why don't you say anything, Mariya? Mariya, why don't you say anything?

MARIYA. It's a matter of principle.

SERAFIMA. For the love of God, what is going on in here? Huh?

MARIYA. Ask Semyon. I'm not talking.

SERAFIMA. Semyon Semyonovich! Semyon Semyonovich! Why don't you say anything, Semyon Semyonovich?

MARIYA. He's being difficult, mama.

SERAFIMA. Semyon Semyonovich, what are you talking in pantomime for? Huh? Semyon Semyonovich.

MARIYA. Senya! Semyon!

SERAFIMA. Semyon Semyonovich.

MARIYA. What if he's had an attack, mama?

SERAFIMA. Oh, come now, Mariya! What makes you think that? No, it couldn't be. Semyon Semyonovich!

MARIYA. I'm going to go look for him, mama.

(Her careful steps are heard in the room)

Senya. Senya! Mama!

SERAFIMA. What happened?

MARIYA. Light the candle.

SERAFIMA. My God, what happened to him?

MARIYA. Just light the candle, I tell you.

SERAFIMA. Where is it? I can't find it.

MARIYA. On the floor, mama. On the floor. Rummage around on the floor, mama. Senya, sweetheart, please don't frighten me. Senya... Mama, what are you doing?

SERAFIMA. I'm crawling, Masha.

MARIYA. Mama, you're crawling in the wrong place. Crawl over there near the rubber plant, the rubber plant.

(All falls silent, and then something falls)

God Almighty, what was that?

SERAFIMA. The rubber plant, Masha. The rubber plant.

MARIYA. I'm going out of my mind, mother, I hope you know that.

SERAFIMA. Wait a minute, Masha, wait a minute. I still haven't crawled over to the chest of drawers. Holy Mother of God, I found it!

MARIYA. Well then, light it, light it.

SERAFIMA. Just a minute, Masha. *(Strikes a match)*

MARIYA. I can't wait any longer, mother. This is torture.

SERAFIMA. *(Runs to Mariya with the candle)* What happened to him?

MARIYA. *(Throws back the blanket)* You see?

SERAFIMA. No.

MARIYA. Me neither.

SERAFIMA. Where is he, then?

MARIYA. He's not here, mama. And the bed's gone cold. Senya... Senya...

He's gone.

SERAFIMA. What do you mean, he's gone?

MARIYA. He's gone. *(Races around the room)* Senya... Senya...

SERAFIMA. *(Holding the candle, peers into the next room)* Semyon Semyonovich!

MARIYA. *(Runs to the bed)* The candle. Bring the candle over here. *(Grabs the candle away from Serafima and puts it on the floor. She gets down on her knees and looks under the bed)* Thank God, right here next to the wall! *(Crawls under the bed)*

SERAFIMA. What are you doing, Masha? Where are you going? Come to your senses!

MARIYA. *(From beneath the bed)* I'm going out, mother. I'm going outside. *(Crawls out from under the bed holding a pair of woman's shoes)* Here they are. *(Begins putting them on)* Give me my skirt, Mama.

(Serafima races over to the bed, puts down the candle and races back towards the chest of drawers)

The candle, leave the candle here. Wait, I'll get it myself. *(Stops Serafima. Runs over to the wall and removes her skirt from the nail it is hanging on)*

SERAFIMA. For God's sake, where are you going, Masha?

MARIYA. I've got to bring him back. I've just got to bring him back. He's in a terrible state. When we were in bed he even showed me one of his symptoms.

SERAFIMA. Mother of God!

MARIYA. You know what?

SERAFIMA. What?

MARIYA. What if he suddenly tries to do something to himself?

SERAFIMA. Why didn't you think of that before, Mariya? Get your shoes on. Quick, get your shoes on.

MARIYA. My blouse! Give me my blouse.

SERAFIMA. Praise be to God! Pants.

MARIYA. What pants?

SERAFIMA. Here are his pants. And if his pants are here, that means he's here.

MARIYA. But what if he left without his pants? He was in a terrible state...

SERAFIMA. A man without pants might as well be a man without eyes. He can't go anywhere.

MARIYA. Well, then, where is he, mama?

SERAFIMA. He must have had to go... you know...

MARIYA. Maybe he'll do something to himself there.

SERAFIMA. What do you mean? Oh, come now.

MARIYA. Simple. Wham!—and it's all over.

SERAFIMA. Holy Mother of God!
MARIYA. What are we going to do? Huh? If he...
SERAFIMA. Shh! Do you hear anything?
MARIYA. No... Do you?
SERAFIMA. I don't either.
MARIYA. Lord what a mess! I'll go knock on the door, mama, come what may.

SCENE FIVE

(Mariya leaves. Serafima turns toward the icon and makes the sign of the cross)

SERAFIMA. *(Crossing herself)* Holy Mothers of Vutivansk, Vatopedsk, Okovitsk, Kupyatitsk, Novo-Nikitsk, Arapetsk, Pskov, Vydropusk, Ogarorusk, Svyatogorsk, Vensk, Svensk, Iversk, Smolensk, Abalatskoe-Znamenie, Bratsk and Kiev, Pimenovsk, Spain and Kazan. Intercede with your Son for the health of my son-in-law. Blessed Mother of God, open unto us thy doors of mercy.

SCENE SIX

(Enter Mariya at a run)

MARIYA. The door is locked. I can't get it open.
SERAFIMA. Did you talk with him?
MARIYA. Yes.
SERAFIMA. Well, what's he doing?
MARIYA. He wouldn't answer my questions and he didn't make any noises.
SERAFIMA. What are we going to do, Masha?
MARIYA. I'll go wake up Alexander Petrovich. He can break down the door.
SERAFIMA. You can't bother Alexander Petrovich.
MARIYA. Why not?
SERAFIMA. Alexander Petrovich is in mourning. He buried his wife last week.
MARIYA. So much the better. He's bound to sympathize with my situation. *(Runs to the door)*
SERAFIMA. I just hope nothing goes wrong, Masha.
MARIYA. One way or another, we need a man. We'll never be able to cope without a man, mama. *(Knocks on the door)* I can't believe it, mother...
SERAFIMA. What?
MARIYA. What what? I don't know what. Anything might happen. You'd better go and listen, mama. Maybe he'll make a noise.

(Serafima leaves)

SCENE SEVEN

(Mariya)

MARIYA. *(Knocks)* Alexander Petrovich... Comrade Kalabushkin... Comrade Kalabushkin...
ALEXANDER. *(From behind the door)* Who's there?
MARIYA. Please don't consider me rude, comrade Kalabushkin. It's me.
ALEXANDER. *(From behind the door)* Huh?
MARIYA. It's me, Podsekalnikova.
ALEXANDER. *(From behind the door)* Who?
MARIYA. Podsekalnikova! Mariya Lukyanovna. Good day to you.
ALEXANDER. *(From behind the door)* What do you want?
MARIYA. I need you terribly, comrade Kalabushkin.
ALEXANDER. *(From behind the door)* What do you mean you need me?
MARIYA. I need a man.
ALEXANDER. *(From behind the door)* What are you saying, Mariya Lukyanovna? Shh!
MARIYA. I realize you're not up to it right now, comrade Kalabushkin. But comrade Kalabushkin, you must understand that I am alone, utterly alone. What else can I do, comrade Kalabushkin?
ALEXANDER. *(From behind the door)* You'd better take a cold shower, Mariya Lukyanovna.
MARIYA. What? Comrade Kalabushkin... Hey, comrade Kalabushkin.
ALEXANDER. *(From behind the door)* Keep it quiet, dammit!
MARIYA. I'm going to have to break the door down, comrade Kalabushkin.
ALEXANDER. For God's sake. Listen to me. Wait a minute. Just wait a minute!

(The door swings open noisily)

SCENE EIGHT

(Margarita, an enormous woman, appears in the doorway in a nightgown)

MARGARITA. Break down the door? Now there's a fine way for a young lady to spend her time. Aren't you a little slut, if you'll pardon the expression.
MARIYA. What do you mean? Please... Alexander Petrovich!
MARGARITA. What are you chasing after Alexander Petrovich for? What kind of filthy business are you up to? We are sitting here together in deepest mourning, reminiscing about the dear departed, and meanwhile you want to break his door down.

MARIYA. You mean you thought I wanted to break down the door? What do you think I am, a crook?

MARGARITA. Modern women are worse than crooks. As God is my witness, they're always looking for something to snitch. Why, you...

ALEXANDER. *(Sticking his head out the door)* Margarita Ivanovna!

MARGARITA. What do you want?

ALEXANDER. If you are planning to beat her up, Margarita Ivanovna, I don't recommend it. Don't forget, you don't officially live here.

(Alexander's head disappears)

MARIYA. Uh, pardon me, but why would you want to do that?

MARGARITA. Why are you chasing after another woman's man?

MARIYA. You seem to have misunderstood me. I assure you. I'm married.

MARGARITA. What's there to understand? I'm married myself.

MARIYA. But, listen. He's going to shoot himself.

ALEXANDER. *(Sticking his head out the door)* Who's going to shoot himself?

MARIYA. Semyon Semyonovich.

ALEXANDER. Where's he going to shoot himself?

MARIYA. Please don't laugh, Alexander Petrovich. In the toilet.

(Alexander's head disappears)

MARGARITA. Who, may I ask, shoots himself in the toilet?

MARIYA. Where else can a man go when he's out of work?

SCENE NINE

(Alexander emerges hurriedly through the door)

ALEXANDER. What the hell are you standing here for? We've got to do something, Mariya Lukyanovna.

MARIYA. That's why I came for you, Alexander Petrovich. You're a militant type, you run a shooting gallery. Help me and my mother break down the door.

ALEXANDER. Why didn't you say so right away?

MARGARITA. What were you waiting for?

ALEXANDER. Come on, Mariya Lukyanovna. We'll sneak up on him and snare him before he knows what hit him. But shh…, like this… on tiptoes.

MARIYA. Shh... *(Tiptoes up to the door)*

(As soon as they are flush with the door, a cry rings out: "Ah!")

ALL. *(Falling back)* Ah!

SCENE TEN

(Serafima runs into the room)

SERAFIMA. Don't go in there! Don't go in there!
MARIYA. Oh, my God!
ALEXANDER. What happened?
SERAFIMA. Picture this, if you will. That wasn't Semyon Semyonovich in there at all. It was the old Volodkina woman from across the hall.
MARIYA. What do you mean, mama?
SERAFIMA. Word of honor. I saw her with my own eyes. She just came out. And there I was, Masha, listening through the door like a damn fool!
ALEXANDER. Looks like we've lost him, Mariya Lukyanovna.
MARIYA. It's your fault, mama. I told you he went out. Alexander Petrovich, I beg you to go out and find him.
SERAFIMA. But how could he go out without his pants? Look here, Alexander Petrovich. His pants are right here.
MARIYA. A man confronting death has no need of pants.
MARGARITA. It depends on where he is, Mariya Lukyanovna. For example, the authorities would never let a man without pants die in the center of town. That I can guarantee you.
ALEXANDER. Have you looked everywhere in the building?
MARIYA. Absolutely everywhere.
SERAFIMA. Except the kitchen.
MARIYA. Except the kitchen, that's right. Let's go look in the kitchen, comrade Kalabushkin.

(They race for the door with Margarita in pursuit)

ALEXANDER. You wait here, Margarita Ivanovna - we'll take care of this together.

(Alexander and Mariya run out)

SCENE ELEVEN

(Serafima and Margarita)

MARGARITA. That's just like him. Always pairing off with somebody. It's a genuine neurotic disorder. Let's go after them.
SERAFIMA. *(Chases after her)* No, what for? Listen. Just wait a minute.

(At that moment the following sounds are heard from the kitchen in the following order: Alexander shouts "Wait!", followed by the slamming of a door, the squeal of Semyon, and finally, the sound of a body hitting the floor. Then, total silence)

97

MARGARITA. Saints alive, what was that?
SERAFIMA. It's all over now. He's shot himself. Shot himself for sure.
MARGARITA. What are we going to do?
SERAFIMA. I think I'm going to scream or something.
MARGARITA. Oh, no, don't.
SERAFIMA. I'm afraid.
MARGARITA. Me, too.
SERAFIMA. Someone's coming!
MARGARITA. Where?
SERAFIMA. They're bringing something.
MARGARITA. What?
SERAFIMA. They're bringing him!
MARGARITA. They're bringing him in here.
SERAFIMA. You're right, they're bringing him in here.
MARGARITA. Oh, my God!
SERAFIMA. Here they come.
MARGARITA. Here they come.
SERAFIMA. What's going to happen? What's going to happen?

SCENE TWELVE

(Alexander drags in the terrified Semyon)

SEMYON. What happened? What happened?
ALEXANDER. Don't you worry, Semyon Semyonovich.
SEMYON. What are you holding me for? What are you doing? Unhand me.
  Let go of me! Let me go!
SERAFIMA. Don't let him go.
MARGARITA. Hold him. Hold him.
SERAFIMA. Where's Masha? Where did Masha go?
ALEXANDER. Your Masha is splayed out on the kitchen floor.
SERAFIMA. What do you mean she's splayed out on the floor?
ALEXANDER. In a very serious faint, Serafima Ilinishna.
SERAFIMA. What is happening to us? Holy saints alive. *(Runs from the room
  with Margarita in pursuit)*

SCENE THIRTEEN

(Alexander and Semyon)
SEMYON. Excuse me, but what are you digging in my pockets for? What do
  you want? Leave me alone, please.
ALEXANDER. First, give me that thing.
SEMYON. What thing? Give you what? I don't have anything. Absolutely

nothing, don't you understand?

ALEXANDER. But I saw you sticking it in your mouth.

SEMYON. That's a lie. I wasn't sticking anything in my mouth. Unhand me. Let me go this instant.

ALEXANDER. All right, I'll leave you alone, Semyon Semyonovich. But give me your word, Semyon Semyonovich, that you won't attempt to do anything to yourself until you have heard me out. I beg you as a friend, Semyon Semyonovich. Just listen to what I have to say.

SEMYON. Go ahead. I'm listening.

ALEXANDER. Thank you. Have a seat, Semyon Semyonovich. *(Seats him and strikes a pose)* Citizen Podsekalnikov... Wait a minute. *(Runs to the window and throws back the curtain. The unhealthy urban morning light illuminates the messy bed, the broken rubber plant, and the whole room's melancholy appearance)* Citizen Podsekalnikov. Life is beautiful.

SEMYON. So what's it to me?

ALEXANDER. What are you talking about? Citizen Podsekalnikov, where do you think you are you living? You are living in the twentieth century. The age of enlightenment. The age of electricity.

SEMYON. And when they turn off the electricity because I can't pay the bills, what kind of age am I left in? The Stone Age?

ALEXANDER. Exactly. The Stone Age, citizen Podsekalnikov. It's as though we've been living in caves for ages. It's enough to make you suicidal. Dammit all! What am I saying? Don't confuse me, citizen Podsekalnikov! Life is beautiful.

SEMYON. I read about that in the newspapers, but I think they'll print a retraction any day now.

ALEXANDER. You're wrong to think like that. Don't think. Work.

SEMYON. The unemployed aren't allowed to work.

ALEXANDER. You're always waiting for permission from someone. You've got to struggle with life, Semyon Semyonovich.

SEMYON. You think I haven't struggled, comrade Kalabushkin? Take a look at this, if you will. *(Pulls a booklet out from beneath the pillow)*

ALEXANDER. What's that?

SEMYON. Instructions for playing the tuba.

ALEXANDER. The what?

SEMYON. The tuba. It makes music. It's a wind instrument that makes heavenly, spiritual sounds. You can learn to play it in twenty lessons. And then it's easy street. I even drew up an estimate. *(Shows a piece of paper)* Approximately twenty concerts a month at five-and-a-half rubles per concert. That makes a yearly income of one thousand, three hundred and twenty rubles. As you can see yourself, comrade Kalabushkin, I am fully prepared to begin playing the tuba. I have the desire, I have the estimate and I have the instructions. The only thing I'm lacking is the horn.

ALEXANDER. You're not the only one, citizen Podsekalnikov. But what can you do? You've got to live on.

SEMYON. No doubt about that, comrade Kalabushkin.

ALEXANDER. You agree?

SEMYON. I agree, comrade Kalabushkin.

ALEXANDER. Then, I've convinced you. Thank you. Hurrah! Give me the revolver, citizen Podsekalnikov.

SEMYON. Revolver? What revolver?

ALEXANDER. There you go again. I saw you sticking it in your mouth.

SEMYON. Me?

ALEXANDER. You.

SEMYON. My God! Me, sticking a revolver in my mouth. What for?

ALEXANDER. Stop trying to make an idiot out of me. Everybody knows you are trying to shoot yourself.

SEMYON. Who's shooting himself?

ALEXANDER. You're shooting yourself.

SEMYON. Me?

ALEXANDER. You.

SEMYON. My God! Wait a minute. Me personally?

ALEXANDER. You personally, citizen Podsekalnikov.

SEMYON. Would you like to tell me why I would want to shoot myself?

ALEXANDER. You mean you don't know yourself?

SEMYON. I am asking you why.

ALEXANDER. Because you haven't worked anywhere for a whole year and you are ashamed to be living off of somebody else's wages. Now isn't that stupid, Semyon Semyonovich?

SEMYON. Wait a minute. Who told you that?

ALEXANDER. Don't worry. It was Mariya Lukyanovna herself.

SEMYON. Ah! Get out of here. Leave me alone. Get the hell out of here!

ALEXANDER. Give me the revolver and I'll leave.

SEMYON. Don't tell me you don't believe me, comrade Kalabushkin. Where could I have gotten a revolver?

ALEXANDER. These days that's no problem. Go see Panfilych and he'll give you a revolver in exchange for a razor.

SEMYON. A razor? Is that so?

ALEXANDER. It's a bad trade, though. It's illegal. If the police show up—wham!—six months hard labor. Give me the revolver, Semyon Semyonovich.

SEMYON. I won't give it to you.

ALEXANDER. Well, don't blame me if you get hurt. I'll just have to take it by force. (Grabs him by the arm) You won't get away from me now.

SEMYON. Is that so? Well, hear this, comrade Kalabushkin. If you don't clear out of here this instant I'll shoot myself before your very eyes.

ALEXANDER. Don't shoot.
SEMYON. You don't believe me? All right, I'll count to three. One...
ALEXANDER. My God, he'd do it!
SEMYON. Two...
ALEXANDER. All right, I'll leave! (*Like a bullet, races into his own room*)

SCENE FOURTEEN

(*Semyon*)

SEMYON. Three. (*Pulls a stick of liverwurst out of his pocket*) Now, where am I going to put this? Where's a plate? (*Puts the liverwurst on a plate*) Just as it was. They'll never notice a thing. All right, Mariya, you just wait. I'll show you. (*Runs to the table, begins shuffling for something*) I'll show you how ashamed I am to live off of your wages. Just you wait. I'll show you. Here it is. (*Pulls out a razor*) My father's Swedish razor. To hell with it. I won't be shaving in this world again. (*Runs out*)
VOICE OF ALEXANDER. Citizen Podsekalnikov, I promise I won't come back out. Only, listen to me. Citizen Podsekalnikov, take my word for it, life is beautiful. Citizen Podse... (*Pokes his head in the door and looks around*) Where is he?

SCENE FIFTEEN

(*Alexander enters from his room and looks around*)

ALEXANDER. He's probably in there. (*Runs to the door*) Citizen Podsekalnikov, whatever you do, don't shoot yourself. I won't come in. Citizen Podsekalnikov, you're probably amazed by my offensive nature, but once again I would like to direct your unwavering attention through this wall, here, to the fact that life is beautiful. Citizen Podsekalnikov...

SCENE SIXTEEN

(*Serafima and Margarita drag in an unconscious Mariya*)

SERAFIMA. What are you doing? What are you doing? Grab her by the feet, Margarita Ivanovna.
MARGARITA. Easy does it. Easy does it.
ALEXANDER. Have you completely lost your minds? What are you dragging a woman like a sack of potatoes for? Put her down on her rear end.

101

SERAFIMA. Now, unbutton her blouse.

ALEXANDER. My pleasure.

MARIYA. Who's there?

ALEXANDER. We're all family, Mariya Lukyanovna. Don't be shy.

MARIYA. Where is he? What happened to him? Is he dead, comrade Kalabushkin?

ALEXANDER. Not quite yet, Mariya Lukyanovna. But I have to tell you that he's working on it.

MARIYA. Let me go to him.

ALEXANDER. Don't even think of it, Mariya Lukyanovna. You'll ruin the whole thing. He told me himself, "If you so much as cross the threshold, I'll shoot myself," he says, "right here before your very eyes."

SERAFIMA. So what did you do?

ALEXANDER. Well, I did what I could. I begged and pleaded, but nothing worked.

MARGARITA. You've got to give orders, not plead. Go report him to the police this instant. Let 'em arrest him and send him to court.

ALEXANDER. There's no such law, Margarita Ivanovna. No court can sentence you to life. Death... yes. Life... no.

SERAFIMA. So what do we do?

ALEXANDER. Get a horn, Serafima Ilinishna.

SERAFIMA. What do you mean, get a horn?

ALEXANDER. There's this horn, Serafima Ilinishna, a b-flat bass flugelhorn or something, and this horn is the salvation to all his problems.

MARIYA. What is he going to do with a horn, if may I ask?

ALEXANDER. Amass money, Mariya Lukyanovna. If we get him a horn, I can guarantee you he won't shoot himself.

SERAFIMA. How much does a horn cost?

ALEXANDER. I imagine five-hundred rubles or more.

MARIYA. Five-hundred rubles? The day we get five-hundred rubles he won't need a horn to keep him from shooting himself.

ALEXANDER. You're probably right, Mariya Lukyanovna.

MARGARITA. I'll have to get my musicians to lend him a horn.

SERAFIMA. You mean you have your own musicians?

ALEXANDER. She has a spectacular orchestra of symphonic music at her restaurant, Serafima Ilinishna.

MARGARITA. They're called "The Free Artists Trio."

SERAFIMA. For God's sake, my dear, have a chat with them.

MARIYA. Please, do ask them.

SERAFIMA. But do it now, and hurry.

MARIYA. I'll go with you, Margarita Ivanovna. Put some clothes on.

(Margarita and Mariya go into Alexander's room)

SCENE SEVENTEEN

(Alexander and Serafima)

SERAFIMA. I'm afraid he won't last until the horn gets here.

ALEXANDER. Serafima Ilinishna, since you're staying here, you distract him until the horn arrives.

SERAFIMA. What do I do to distract him?

ALEXANDER. I suggest the following, Serafima Ilinishna. Just go into the other room and start carrying on shamelessly. Pretend that you don't have a clue about anything and start telling him stories.

SERAFIMA. What stories?

ALEXANDER. Anything distracting. About the good life. Happy things. Something funny.

SERAFIMA. I don't know anything like that, comrade Kalabushkin.

ALEXANDER. Well, I don't either, but think of something. Your son-in-law's on the edge, Serafima Ilinishna. This is no laughing matter. Tell him some jokes or something, or make up a funny story. Make him forget himself for a moment, distract him, confuse him. We'll hurry it up with the tuba and a man's life will be saved, Serafima Ilinishna. Well, go on. Don't be afraid. Tell him anything. *(Exits to his own room)*

SCENE EIGHTEEN

(Serafima stops before the door)

SERAFIMA. My God, what am I going to tell him? Well, here goes nothing. *(Exits to her own room)*

SCENE NINETEEN

(Enter Semyon. He looks around furtively. Takes a revolver from his pocket and loads it with a cartridge. Sits on the table and opens the ink well. Tears off a sheet of paper)

SEMYON. *(Writes)* "In the event of my death..."

SCENE TWENTY

(Serafima enters from her room)

SERAFIMA. He's not there. *(Notices Semyon)* Lord Almighty! Good morning to you, Semyon Semyonovich. Oh, have I got a story to tell you. You'll just die laughing. Did you ever hear the one about the Germans?

SEMYON. No. What about 'em?

SERAFIMA. Some Germans ate a live pug.

SEMYON. What Germans?

SERAFIMA. Well, I don't remember, but they ate a pug. My late husband used to tell about it. That was in peacetime, Semyon Semyonovich. We all darn near died laughing. *(Pause)* A pug is a dog, you know, Semyon Semyonovich.

SEMYON. So?

SERAFIMA. People don't eat dogs.

SEMYON. So?

SERAFIMA. Well, the Germans ate one.

SEMYON. So?

SERAFIMA. That's all.

SEMYON. What's all?

SERAFIMA. Lord Almighty, now what do I tell him? Here's another funny one in the same vein.

SEMYON. I wish you would leave, Serafima Ilinishna.

SERAFIMA. This one'll kill you, Semyon Semyonovich.

SEMYON. Don't bother me. You might have noticed that I'm busy.

SERAFIMA. No, no. Listen here. Picture this. It was during the war and there was this Turkish prisoner in the village. They took him captive. Well, naturally, his head was bashed in. Our soldiers had rung his bell pretty good. It was so bad his head kept shaking like this. Everybody died laughing. So what did they do? Every evening, everybody in town would get together. Somebody would bring bread, somebody else would bring meat-jelly, and they'd set off to see the prisoner. They'd dangle the food in front of him and say, "You want to eat?" Well the Turk was dying for some of that Russian meat jelly, but he didn't know a word of Russian. Well, he'd just jump up, and he was starving so bad his whole body was shaking. And his head would start shaking back and forth like he's saying "no." Well, that's just what everybody was waiting for and they'd start wrapping all the food back up. "If you don't want anything, that's fine with us," they'd say, and then they'd all go back home. God how they laughed at that Turk. What do you say to that one?

SEMYON. Get the hell out of here. You understand me?

SERAFIMA. What's the matter, Semyon Semyonovich? And then there's the one about the coronation.

(Semyon leaps up, grabs a pen, paper and ink)

Wait. Wait. Where are you going, Semyon Semyonovich? *(She chases after him)* Blessed Alexander cornered a Jew in the palace entryway.

(Semyon runs into the next room)

SCENE TWENTY-ONE

(Serafima, alone before the door)

SERAFIMA. I didn't distract him. Where can I come up with some more jokes? Lord Almighty! *(Runs after him)*

SCENE TWENTY-TWO

(Enter Alexander, Mariya, and Margarita from Alexander's room)

ALEXANDER. Hurry it up, Margarita Ivanovna!
MARIYA. Maybe we shouldn't leave Senya alone.
ALEXANDER. Don't worry, Mariya Lukyanovna. He's with your mother. I told her how to handle him.

(They run out)

SCENE TWENTY-THREE

(Semyon rushes in from the neighboring room, holding the ink well, pen and paper)

SEMYON. *(Shouts at the door)* If you try telling me about the pug-dog again, I'll skin you alive. Leave me alone, you damned old idiot. *(Slams the door. Approaches the table, spreads out the paper and finishes writing)* "I blame no one. Podsekalnikov."

END OF ACT I

ACT II

(Same room as in Act I. All has been tidied up)

SCENE ONE

(Semyon sits on a stool with an enormous tuba positioned on his shoulder. An instruction booklet lies open before him. Mariya and Serafima sit on two chairs off to the side)

SEMYON. *(Reads)* "Chapter One. 'How to Play.' In order to play the bass tuba one must apply the proper three finger combination. The first finger is applied to the first valve. The second finger is applied to the second valve. The third finger is applied to the third valve." All right. "Upon exhalation the note 'B-flat' shall be achieved." *(Blows. Blows again)* What the hell kind of surprise is this? All air and no sound.

SERAFIMA. Look out, now, Mariya. If he loses faith in this horn...

SEMYON. Wait, wait, wait! Here we are. Here's a chapter specially about the exhalation of air. It's called, "How to Blow." "In order to exhale properly, I, the world-famous artist of sound, Theodore Hugo Schultz, propose a simple and inexpensive method. Tear off a piece of yesterday's newspaper and place it on the tongue."

SERAFIMA. On the tongue?

SEMYON. On the tongue, Serafima Ilinishna. So. Give me a newspaper.

(Serafima runs up with a newspaper)

Tear off a piece.

MARIYA. Not so big, mama. Not so big.

SEMYON. Now, put it on my tongue, Serafima Ilinishna.

SERAFIMA. Well. Did that help, Semyon Semyonovich?

SEMYON. Ee-a-i-i-i-a-a. Ee-a-i-i-i-a-a, a-e-u.

MARIYA. What?

SEMYON. I-ee-a.

MARIYA. What?

SEMYON. I-ee-a, a-e-u.

MARIYA. What are you saying, Senya sweetheart? I can't understand a word.

SEMYON. *(Spits out the newspaper)* Idiot, I said. Now do you understand me?

106

I told you in plain Russian, "Read a little bit further." Tear off a corner of yesterday's newspaper and place it on the tongue. And then what?

MARIYA. Then, Senya, it says, *(Reads)* "Spit the piece of paper on the floor. Try to remember the exact position the tongue assumes during the act of expectoration. Having fixed the prescribed position, blow just as you spit." That's all.

SEMYON. I demand silence and attention. *(Tears off a corner of the newspaper)* Please stand aside, Serafima Ilinishna. *(Puts it on his tongue. Spits. Begins blowing)* What the hell is this? Not a sound.

SERAFIMA. It's all over, now. He's starting to get disillusioned.

(Semyon spits again. Prepares to blow)

MARIYA. Dear Lord! If you truly do exist, please send him a sound.

(At that very instant the entire room is filled with the deafening roar of the tuba)

SERAFIMA. God exists! I told you all along. There's cash on the barrel head for you.

SEMYON. All right, Mariya, hand in your resignation. You won't be working anymore.

MARIYA. How's that?

SERAFIMA. What are we going to live on?

SEMYON. I figured it all out in advance. Approximately twenty concerts a month at five-and-a-half rubles a concert. That gives me a yearly income of... Wait a second. *(Rummages in his pocket)* I've got the figures right here someplace. *(Pulls out a piece of paper)* Here they are. Listen. *(Unfolds a piece of paper and reads)* "In the event of my..." *(Pause)* Wait a minute. That's not it. *(Hides the paper. Pulls out another)* Here it is. Right here. In black and white. "I shall realize a yearly income of one thousand, three hundred and twenty rubles." That's right. And you ask, what are we going to live on.

SERAFIMA. But you still haven't learned how to play, Semyon Semyon-ovich.

SEMYON. Learning is as easy as spitting, now, Serafima Ilinishna. *(Picks up some paper. Spits. Blows. The tuba roars)* Did you hear that? This tuba is the ticket to a life in clover, Serafima Ilinishna. Masha, just imagine how grand it will be to come home from a concert with a sack of money and sit down on the sofa surrounded by my happy family. "So, did they polish the floor today?" "They certainly did, Semyon Semyonovich." "And did you buy that statue I had my eye on?" "Yes, we bought the statue, too, Semyon Semyonovich." "Marvelous. Now, bring me some egg-nog." That's what I call living. By the way, from this moment forth I demand that you serve me the aforementioned egg-nog for dessert every day. First of all, egg-nog clears the chest, and second of all, I like egg-nog. Is that understood?

MARIYA. Eggs are expensive, Senya.

SEMYON. Expensive for who? Who does that concern besides me? Who's the breadwinner now, you or me?

SERAFIMA. But...

SEMYON. You are constantly interrupting my planning sessions. Quit contradicting me, Serafima Ilinishna. You'd be better off listening to some music. *(Blows)* And, in general, I demand relative quiet during moments of creative inspiration. *(Reads)* "'The Scale.' The scale is the belly-button of music. Your mastering of this belly-button signifies your birth as a musician." Well, now I can finally get down to learning the rest. "In order to learn the scale properly, I, the world-famous artist of sound, Theodore Hugo Schultz, propose to you the most inexpensive method. Buy yourself a cheap pi... *(Turns the page)* ...ano." What piano?

SERAFIMA and MARIYA. Piano?

SEMYON. Wait a minute, here. That's not possible. "I propose to you the most inexpensive method. Buy yourself the cheapest pi... *(Checks to see whether the pages aren't stuck together)* ...ano." What's that supposed to mean? What's a piano got to do with it? *(Reads)* "Consult the footnotes for the proper method of playing the scale. Play the scale on the piano and then repeat it on the tuba." What's going on here, comrades? What is going on? Then, it's all over. It's all over. This guy is a scoundrel! And he calls himself an artist of sound. You're no artist, Theodore, you're a bum. You're a crook, you and your belly-button. *(Rips up the instruction booklet)* Masha! Masha! Serafima Ilinishna! I've got nothing to buy a piano with. What has he done to me? I considered him my saviour! I considered this tuba my eye-glass to the future...

SERAFIMA. Calm down, Semyon Semyonovich. Forget it.

SEMYON. How are we going to live, Serafima Ilinishna? Masha, who's going to support us now?

MARIYA. Don't even think about it, Senya. I'll support us alone.

SERAFIMA. Look how long we lived on Masha's salary alone. We'll just go on that way.

SEMYON. Oh, so you think we've only been living off of Masha's salary? You mean to say I'm worthless here, Serafima Ilinishna? Well, there's one thing you haven't taken into account, Serafima Ilinishna. She had everything else supplied for her from the beginning. Who bought these glasses, Serafima Ilinishna? I bought them. And who bought these saucers, Serafima Ilinishna? I bought them. And when these saucers break, Mariya, can you afford to buy new ones?

MARIYA. Yes, Senya, yes.

SEMYON. You can?

MARIYA. Yes.

SEMYON. *(Throws a saucer on the floor, breaking it)* Well, we'll see about that. And when these glasses break, Mariya, can you afford to buy new ones?

MARIYA. Oh my God, no!

SEMYON. You can't? Well then, we can't live like this. There's only one thing left for me to do... Get out of here. This instant, I tell you. A salary like yours can't support three people.

MARIYA. What are you saying, Senya sweetheart? There's enough for us and for you too.

SEMYON. How can there be enough for me, Mariya, if there isn't even enough to buy glasses with?

MARIYA. There's enough, Senya, there's enough.

SEMYON. There is? *(Smashes the glasses)* We'll see about that. And when this vase breaks, Mariya, can you afford to buy a new one?

SERAFIMA. Tell him you can't.

MARIYA. No, Senya.

SEMYON. Oh, so you can't! Then get out of here right now.

MARIYA. Kill me if you want, but I won't go.

SEMYON. You won't go?

MARIYA. I won't go.

SEMYON. We'll see about that. *(Smashes the vase)*

MARIYA. Senya, are you going to smash everything?

SEMYON. Everything.

MARIYA. Everything?

SEMYON. Everything.

MARIYA. We'll see about that. *(Smashes the mirror)*

SEMYON. You... in my presence... the head of the... What is happening? My God! For God's sake, leave me alone. I beg of you. For God's sake, leave me alone. Please.

(Mariya and Serafima go into the other room. Semyon closes the door behind them)

SCENE TWO

(Semyon alone)

SEMYON. Everything is ruined... glasses... saucers... human life... Life is ruined and there's no one to lament it. The world... The universe... Mankind... A grave... and a couple of people standing over it. That's all there is to mankind. *(Goes to the table)* Look how long we've lived on Masha's pay, and we'll go on that way. *(Opens a drawer)* We'll just go on that way. *(Takes out a revolver)* Or, maybe not. *(Takes a note out of his pocket and puts it on the table)* Maybe not. *(Jumps up)* No, damn it, we won't go on! *(Puts the revolver to his head. His gaze falls on the note. He lowers his hand and picks up the note. Reads)* "I shall realize a yearly income of one thousand, three hundred and twenty rubles." *(Tears up the note. Pulls out another and puts it on the table. Again raises the revolver to his head)* There's egg-nog for you, Senya. *(Squints. Suddenly there is a deafening knock at the door. Semyon hides the revolver behind his back)* Yes? Who's there?

(The door swings open and Aristarkh enters)

SCENE THREE

(Aristarkh and Semyon with the revolver behind his back)

ARISTARKH. I beg your pardon. Perhaps I'm intruding? Please do excuse me. If you were doing something, by all means, please do go on.

SEMYON. No, no. I'm in no hurry. Who are..., uh, what can I do for you?

ARISTARKH. Perhaps you'll tell me first with whom I have the pleasant honor of speaking?

SEMYON. With, uh, what's-his-name... Podsekalnikov.

ARISTARKH. Very happy to meet you. Allow me to inquire, are you the same Podsekalnikov who is planning to shoot himself?

SEMYON. Who told you? That is, no. Just a slip there. Now they'll arrest me for keeping a firearm. I'm not him. Really, I'm not him.

ARISTARKH. Is that so? But how is that possible? I have the right address and... *(Notices the note)* Wait a minute. *(Picks up the note)* You see it's written right here, *(Reads)* "In the event of my death, I blame no one." And it is signed, "Podsekalnikov." Is that you, Podsekalnikov?

SEMYON. Me. Six months hard labor.

ARISTARKH. Now, see here. That's impossible, entirely impossible, citizen Podsekalnikov. Tell me, if you please, what good does it do anyone to blame no one? On the contrary, you must accuse and blame, citizen Podsekalnikov. You are shooting yourself. Splendid. Beautiful. Shoot yourself in good health. Only, please, shoot yourself as a social activist. Don't forget you are not alone, citizen Podsekalnikov. Look around you. Take a look at our intelligentsia. What do you see? A great deal. What do you hear? Nothing. Why do you hear nothing? Because the intelligentsia is silent. Why do you think it is silent? Because it is forced to be silent. But you can't force a dead man to be silent, citizen Podsekalnikov. That is, if a dead man decides to speak. In times like ours, citizen Podsekalnikov, only a dead man can say what a live man thinks. And I have come to you as if to a dead man, citizen Podsekalnikov. I have come to you in the name of the Russian intelligentsia.

SEMYON. Pleased to meet you. Won't you have a seat?

ARISTARKH. You are parting with life, citizen Podsekalnikov. And on that

110

score you are correct. Living is truly impossible. However, someone must be to blame for that. And if I can't talk about it, citizen Podsekalnikov, you can. You have nothing to lose. You have nothing to fear. You are free now, citizen Podsekalnikov. So speak up honestly, openly and bravely, citizen Podsekalnikov. Whom do you accuse?

SEMYON. Me?

ARISTARKH. Yes.

SEMYON. Theodore Hugo Schultz.

ARISTARKH. Someone from the Communist International, I presume? Doubtless he is to blame, too. But he is not alone, citizen Podsekalnikov. You foolishly accuse only him. Accuse them all. I fear that you still don't understand properly why you are shooting yourself. Allow me to explain it for you.

SEMYON. Please do. That would be very kind of you.

ARISTARKH. You want to perish for the sake of truth, citizen Podsekalnikov.

SEMYON. There's an idea for you.

ARISTARKH. Only the truth does not wait, citizen Podsekalnikov. You must perish quickly. Tear up your note this instant and write a new one. Be sincere and name everyone who deserves it. And defend us in it. Defend the intelligentsia and challenge the state with the following merciless question. In all of their constructive work, why have they not utilized the services of such an obviously sensitive, loyal, and knowledgeable person as Aristarkh Dominikovich Grand-Skubik.

SEMYON. Who?

ARISTARKH. Aristarkh Dominikovich Grand-Skubik. That's written with a dash.

SEMYON. Who is that?

ARISTARKH. Me. And when you have written this note, citizen Podsekalnikov, you will shoot yourself. You will shoot yourself as a hero. Your shot will be heard throughout all of Russia. It will wake the nation's slumbering conscience. It will serve as an alarm to the makers of public opinion. Your name will be on everyone's lips. Your death will become the hottest theme of public disputations. Your portrait will be printed in news- papers and your name will become a slogan, citizen Podsekalnikov.

SEMYON. Hey, I like that, Aristarkh Dominikovich. Go on. Go on. Tell me more, Aristarkh Dominikovich.

ARISTARKH. The entire Russian intelligentsia will gather at your grave, citizen Podsekalnikov. The nation's finest will carry you out into the street. You will be buried in wreaths, citizen Podsekalnikov. Your bier will be drowning in flowers, and splendid horses in white horsecloths will bear you to the cemetery, citizen Podsekalnikov.

SEMYON. Holy Moses! Now that's what I call living!

ARISTARKH. I myself would shoot myself, citizen Podsekalnikov, but unfortunately I can't. It's a matter of principle. *(Looks at his watch)* So. Here's what we'll do. You draw up an outline for a suicide note... Or perhaps I should do it myself and you merely sign it and shoot yourself.

SEMYON. What for? I'll write it myself.

ARISTARKH. You are Pozharsky. You are Minin, citizen Podsekalnikov.[1] You are a titan. Allow me to embrace you in the name of the Russian intelligentsia. *(Embraces him)* I didn't weep when my own mother passed away. My own poor mother, citizen Podsekalnikov. And now... and now... *(Leaves weeping)*

SCENE FOUR

(Semyon alone)

SEMYON. I will suffer. I will suffer for all. Splendid horses in white horsecloths. I definitely will suffer. Where's some paper? *(Looks around)* I'll expose all of them. Where's some paper? I'll accuse everybody. *(Looks around)* Now you've had it. You can all shake in your boots. I'll write the whole truth. And nothing but the truth. Because I know more truth than is good for me. *(Looks around)* What the hell? They call this living? You finally find the truth and there's no paper to write it down on. *(Goes to the door and opens it)* I am leaving.

SCENE FIVE

(Mariya and Serafima enter at a run)

MARIYA. Where are you going?

SEMYON. To get some paper. For the truth. Give me my hat and a ruble, Serafima Ilinishna. And Masha, I must have a word with you. Look at yourself. Look at yourself, will you? This can't go on. I have guests. Members of the intelligentsia. We have to keep up appearances, Masha.

MARIYA. What do you think I need to do, Senya?

SEMYON. Stick a pin or something on your blouse, or at the very least try washing your hair. Don't forget that you bear the name Podsekalnikov. That entails a thing or two, you know.

(Serafima gives him his hat and a ruble)

Now, get yourselves to the kitchen.

---

[1] Dmitry Pozharsky and Kuzma Minin are national heroes for their part in defending the Russian state from Polish interventionists in the early 17th century. In order to avoid obscurity in performance, these first two sentences might be replaced by, "You are a hero, a national hero, citizen Podsekalnikov."

(Exit Mariya and Serafima)

SCENE SIX

(Semyon puts on his hat, examines himself in the broken fragment of mirror)

SEMYON. I do bear a resemblance to Pozharsky, don't I? And there's even a little Minin in me. But I'd say there's more Pozharsky than Minin.[2]

SCENE SEVEN

SERAFIMA. *(Poking out her head)* Some lady has come to see you, Semyon Semyonovich.
SEMYON. Let her in.

SCENE EIGHT

(Enter Cleopatra)

CLEOPATRA. Are you monsieur Podsekalnikov?
SEMYON. Oui, madame. Me personally.
CLEOPATRA. Make my acquaintance. *(Holds out her hand)* Cleopatra Maximovna. But you can simply call me Capochka.
SEMYON. My goodness!
CLEOPATRA. And now that we're acquainted, I would like to ask a small favor of you.
SEMYON. Of course. Please do. How may I help you?
CLEOPATRA. Mister Podsekalnikov, you're planning to shoot yourself anyway, so be a darling and shoot yourself for me.
SEMYON. What do you mean, for you?
CLEOPATRA. Don't be so egotistical, monsieur Podsekalnikov. Shoot yourself for my sake.
SEMYON. Unfortunately I can't. I'm already promised to someone else.
CLEOPATRA. To whom? Raisa Filippovna? Oh, how could you? What is the matter with you, monsieur Podsekalnikov! If you shoot yourself for the sake of that piece of trash, Oleg Leonidovich will drop me like a hot rock. You'd do better to shoot yourself for me and then Oleg Leonidovich will drop her like a hot rock. Because Oleg Leonidovich is an aesthete and Raisa Filippovna is simply a bitch. I tell you this because I am a romantic. She even gnaws on glasses when she gets excited. She wants him to kiss her body. She herself wants to kiss his body. Body, body, body, nothing but body. I, on the other hand, only want to worship his soul. I want him to

---

[2] If, in performance, the lines referring to Minin and Pozharsky in scene three above are replaced, these lines may be replaced by, "Yes, I do have the look of a Russian hero, don't I?"

worship my soul. Soul, soul, soul, nothing but soul. Defend the soul, mister Podsekalnikov, shoot yourself for my sake. Resurrect love. Resurrect romance. And then... hundreds of young girls will gather at your grave, monsieur Podsekalnikov. Hundreds of youths will carry you on their tender shoulders. And beautiful women...

SEMYON. ...In white horsecloths.

CLEOPATRA. What?

SEMYON. Pardon me. I got carried away, Cleopatra Maximovna.

CLEOPATRA. What? Already? You are a madman, monsieur Podsekalnikov. No, no, no! Don't kiss me, please!

SEMYON. I assure you...

CLEOPATRA. I believe you, I believe you. But now it's obvious that you have to reject Raisa Filippovna.

SEMYON. I've never even seen any Raisa Filippovna.

CLEOPATRA. You haven't? Then you will. You'll see that you'll see her. She may even show up any minute now. She'll probably tell you that everyone is just crazy about her stomach. She tells that to everyone everywhere. Only it's not true, monsieur Podsekalnikov. She has a very ordinary stomach. I assure you. And anyway, a stomach isn't a face. Even when you're kissing it, you can't make out what it looks like. But a face... Come over here. Have you noticed?

SEMYON. No.

CLEOPATRA. What do you mean, no? Monsieur Podsekalnikov, if you can't tell that I am gorgeous in the face, then come away with me to my place and you will definitely see it. I have a photograph hanging over my bed. You won't believe it. The instant you see it you'll cry out, "Cleopatra Maximovna, you are a beauty!"

SEMYON. You don't say.

CLEOPATRA. I assure you. You'll be stunned. Well, let's go, let's go, monsieur Podsekalnikov. You can finish writing over coffee at my place.

SEMYON. What do you mean finish writing? Writing what?

CLEOPATRA. Everything that you feel. That I crushed you with my charms and that you have no hope of seeing your love reciprocated, and, for that reason, alas, you are shooting yourself. I feel rather odd coaxing you along, mister Podsekalnikov. After all, you are an aesthete yourself. You are a romantic, aren't you?

SCENE NINE

(Enter Mariya holding a basin with water, some soap and a scrub brush)

CLEOPATRA. You've got to vacate the premises anyway, monsieur Podsekalnikov. They've come to mop the floor.

MARIYA. I'm not mopping the floor, I'm washing my hair.

114

CLEOPATRA. I wasn't talking to you, dearie. Who is this vulgar woman?
SEMYON. That's... that's...

(Mariya passes into the next room)

My cook, Cleopatra Maximovna.

SCENE TEN

(Enter Serafima with a broom and dust pan)

SERAFIMA. Where are you going? The samovar is boiling. Perhaps the lady
  would like some tea?
SEMYON. Listen, sweetie. Why don't you just tidy up the place? The lady
  and I are going out for coffee. This is, uh, the cook's mother, Cleopatra
  Maximovna. Come on, let's go. *(Exit Semyon and Cleopatra)*

SCENE ELEVEN

(Mariya and Serafima)

SERAFIMA. Thank God, Masha, it all blew over. You don't have to worry
  about Senya anymore.
MARIYA. I can't help but worry. Even as I stand here taking my bath, I'm
  beside myself. I'm all nerves.
SERAFIMA. Who cares about your nerves when there's a good twelve rubles
  of broken dishes lying around here? Now that's something to worry about.
  And what beautiful crystal it was, too. Here, under the table. Under the
  bed. Lordy, Lordy. *(She crawls under the bed and begins sweeping up the broken
  glass)*

SCENE TWELVE

*(Enter Yegor. He looks around and sees no one. Hearing Mariya's gurgling and
the sounds of splashing water, he sneaks up to the door on tiptoe and peeks through
the crack in the door. Serafima crawls out from under the bed)*

SERAFIMA. What kind of pornography are you up to, young man? There's
  a woman in there washing her hair, or maybe even something worse, and
  there you go trying to sneak a peek.
YEGOR. But, Serafima Ilinishna, I am peeking at her from a Marxist point of
  view, and from that point of view nothing is pornographic.
SERAFIMA. You mean things look differently from that point of view?
YEGOR. Not only differently, but entirely the opposite. I've tested it myself
  many times. You go walking down the, you know, the boulevard, and
  some dame is walking straight at you. Well, naturally, all dames have all

kinds of curves and shapes. The beauty of it is unbearable and all you can do is squint your eyes and suck in your belly. That's when you've got to catch yourself and think: "I," Serafima Ilinishna, "will look at her from a Marxist point of view...." And then you do it. And what do you think happens, Serafima Ilinishna? That dame loses everything just like that. In the blink of an eye she becomes such a horse face I can't even describe it. These days I don't envy anything. I look at everything from a Marxist point of view. If you want me to, Serafima Ilinishna, I can look at you like that, too.

SERAFIMA. Hallowed saints preserve us!

YEGOR. I'll do it anyway.

SERAFIMA. Help!

SCENE THIRTEEN

(Serafima, Yegor and Mariya)

MARIYA. What's the matter?

SERAFIMA. Yegor's point of view.[3]

MARIYA. What do you mean, mama? What point of view?

YEGOR. Believe it or not, Mariya Lukyanovna, a Marxist point of view.

MARIYA. Are you here on business or pleasure, Yegorushka?

YEGOR. I have come about a comma, Mariya Lukyanovna.

MARIYA. A comma? What do you mean?

YEGOR. Mariya Lukyanovna, I've become a writer and I wrote a composition for the newspaper. Only I don't know where to put the commas.

MARIYA. Congratulations! When's the wedding?

YEGOR. What wedding, Mariya Lukyanovna?

MARIYA. Well, if you've become a writer, you've fallen in love, haven't you? The muse has visited you, Yegorushka.

YEGOR. I'll admit she has, Mariya Lukyanovna.

MARIYA. So who is she, who is she? What's her name, Yegorushka?

YEGOR. My muse?

MARIYA. Yes.

YEGOR. Alexander Petrovich Kalabushkin.

SERAFIMA. That does it. He's flipped his lid.

YEGOR. That's true, Serafima Ilinishna. Ever since I was born I never planned on being a writer, but as soon as I laid eyes on him—boom!—it hit me. He fills me with so much inspiration, Mariya Lukyanovna, that my hand starts twitching on its own. And it writes and writes and writes and writes.

---

[3] In Russian this is an untranslatable pun which continues the theme of "point of view" while introducing the meaning of "Yegor has reached the end of his rope."

SERAFIMA. What's so inspiring about him, Yegorushka?

YEGOR. His eroticism, Serafima Ilinishna. I wrote all about it for the newspaper.

MARIYA. What did you write, Yegorushka?

YEGOR. If you'll tell me where the commas go, I'll read you the whole thing. It goes like this: *(Reads)* "Dear Citizen Editor of our newspaper from a courier employed in a Soviet establishment. Scholars have proven that there are spots on the sun. Alexander Kalabushkin, the keeper of the weights, the muscle-meter and the shooting gallery "The Red Beau-Monde" in the summer garden, is just such a spot in a sexual relation. The muscle-meter has no significance for couriers because we have already measured our strength in the workers' civil war for freedom. But as for the shooting gallery, the shooting gallery is closed and has not been open all summer long. The shooting gallery is closed and couriers want to shoot. Meanwhile, Alexander Petrovich Kalabushkin spends every evening in absentia sitting in a restaurant like a horny buck with Margarita Ivanovna Peresvetova. May the editor rip out his sexual profligacy with his iron hand." And it is signed, "Thirty-five thousand couriers."

MARIYA. You mean you got thirty-five thousand couriers to sign that?

YEGOR. No, I signed it alone.

SERAFIMA. Then why do you sign it "thirty-five thousand couriers?"

YEGOR. That's my pseudonym, Serafima Ilinishna.

SERAFIMA. You've completely flipped, Yegor Timofeyevich. You should be ashamed. You could do a man in for no good reason at all.

SCENE FOURTEEN

(Enter Alexander and Margarita at a run)

ALEXANDER. Is your husband here, Mariya Lukyanovna?

MARIYA. You're just in time. Quick, comrade Kalabushkin. This is Yegor. Please, have a talk with him.

ALEXANDER. Why certainly. What can I do for you, Yegor Timofeyevich?

YEGOR. Well, this, comrade Kalabushkin: "...spends every evening in absentia sitting in a restaurant like a horny buck." Where do you think the comma goes?

ALEXANDER. Before "sitting."

YEGOR. Before "sitting." Merci. I'm off to the newspaper. *(Exits at a run)*

SCENE FIFTEEN

(Mariya, Serafima, Alexander and Margarita)

MARIYA. What have you done? You just eradicated a man's illiteracy. But you know what you really destroyed? Your own head, Alexander

Petrovich. Don't you realize who that horny buck is?

ALEXANDER. No. Who?

MARIYA. None other than you.

ALEXANDER. Me?

MARGARITA. Don't try to wriggle out of this one. Who was the slut you were with this time?

ALEXANDER. It was probably you, Margarita Ivanovna.

SERAFIMA. Yes, you, it was you.

MARIYA. That's right. He wrote about you and the shooting gallery, Margarita Ivanovna.

ALEXANDER. After him! Bring him back! And tell him I'll open the shooting gallery. After him, after him, or we'll never catch him! *(Mariya and Serafima rush out)*

SCENE SIXTEEN

(Alexander and Margarita)

ALEXANDER. What are you going to do?

MARGARITA. Everything will be all right. Don't worry, I won't let you down. Come on, let's go reminisce about your late departed.

(They exit to Alexander's room)

SCENE SEVENTEEN

(Enter Nikifor Arsentyevich Pugachyov, a butcher)

PUGACHYOV. How about that. No one here.

SCENE EIGHTEEN

(Enter Viktor, a writer)

VIKTOR. Is that you, citizen Podsekalnikov?

PUGACHYOV. No. I'm waiting for him myself.

VIKTOR. I see. Um-hm.

SCENE NINETEEN

(Enter Father Yelpidy, a priest)

YELPIDY. Pardon me. Is that you Podsekalnikov?

VIKTOR. No, not I.

YELPIDY. Then it must be you.

PUGACHYOV. Me neither.

SCENE TWENTY

(Enter Aristarkh)

YELPIDY. This must be him. Is that you, Podsekalnikov?
ARISTARKH. My God, no.

SCENE TWENTY-ONE

(Enter Alexander from his room. All race to him)

ARISTARKH. Alexander Petrovich!
PUGACHYOV. Comrade Kalabushkin!

SCENE TWENTY-TWO

(Raisa flies into the room like a whirlwind)

RAISA. So here's where you are, comrade Kalabushkin! Give me back my
    fifteen rubles!
ALEXANDER. Not in front of everyone, Raisa Filippovna!
RAISA. What kind of hocus-pocus are you trying to pull? You deceived me,
    comrade Kalabushkin! You thought you'd pull a fast one with your
    Podsekalnikov. What did I give you fifteen rubles for? So he would shoot
    himself for that other scum? What did you promise me, comrade Kalabush-
    kin? You promised me I could use him, but Cleopatra Maximovna is using
    him instead.
VIKTOR. Pardon me. Who is Cleopatra Maximovna? You promised him to
    me, comrade Kalabushkin.
YELPIDY. You promised him to this man, comrade Kalabushkin? Then what
    did I pay you for?
ALEXANDER. Comrades, what are you really buying when you purchase a
    lottery ticket? A chance at fate. Participation in a calculated risk, comrades.
    And so it is in the present case with Podsekalnikov. Our memorable corpse
    is still alive for now, but we have a huge number of suicide notes. You're
    not the only ones, you know. For example, here are some of the notes so far:
    "I am a sacrificial lamb for nationalists. The Jews did me in." "I can't go on
    because the tax collector is such a viper." "In the event of my death I beg you
    blame no one other than our dear, beloved Soviet state." And so on and so
    forth. We will present all the suicide notes to him, but I can't say which one
    he will select, comrades.
ARISTARKH. Might I say, comrades, he's already chosen. He shall shoot

119

himself in the name of the intelligentsia. I just recently spoke with him about it in person.

ALEXANDER. That is impertinence, Aristarkh Dominikovich. You were supposed to have done all your business through me, like all the other clients.

ARISTARKH. Find your clients another corpse. They can wait.

ALEXANDER. No, you wait.

ARISTARKH. The Russian intelligentsia is in no position to wait any longer.

PUGACHYOV. Comrades, how much longer do you think our commerce can wait?

VIKTOR. What about exalted art?

YELPIDY. And what about our religion?

RAISA. What about love? Love these days is silent. When men make love they don't say anything at all. They just breathe heavily. I know what I'm talking about. They only breathe heavily. I beg you to think about what that means, comrades.

ARISTARKH. No, dear comrades, better to think about our intelligentsia. These days our intelligentsia is nothing but a white slave in the harem of the proletariat.

PUGACHYOV. Well, in that case, these days commerce is a black slave in the harem of the proletariat.

VIKTOR. Well, in that case, art these days is a red slave in the harem of the proletariat.

PUGACHYOV. Why do you keep talking about art, art, art? These days commerce is also an art.

VIKTOR. And why do you keep talking about commerce, commerce, commerce? These days art is also commerce. I mean, writers are forced to live a musical life. We sit confined within the borders of our state at our own personal desks and do nothing but compose fanfares. Fanfares for visiting dignitaries, fanfares for the bosses. I want to be a Tolstoy, not a drummer.

ARISTARKH. We merely want someone to listen to us a bit. To take us seriously, dear comrades.

YELPIDY. We must capture the imagination of the youth.

ARISTARKH. But how?

VIKTOR. How? With ideas.

ARISTARKH. But think how it used to be done. It used to be that people had an idea they wanted to die for. These days the people who want to die don't have any ideas, and the people who have ideas don't want to die. That is something we must struggle against. Now more than ever we need dead ideologists.

YELPIDY. Let this dead man be grist for our mill.

PUGACHYOV. You mean to say ours.

VIKTOR. That's right, ours, but not yours.

ARISTARKH. Why yours and not ours?

VIKTOR. Because ours and not yours.

YELPIDY. No, ours.

PUGACHYOV. No, ours.

ALEXANDER. Silence, silence comrades! You're all milling the same grain, what's to argue about? You should join together and make common use of him.

RAISA. One measly dead man for all of us?

VIKTOR. The dead man, as such, isn't what's important. What's important is what's left after him.

PUGACHYOV. There won't be anything left.

VIKTOR. Yes, there will.

PUGACHYOV. What would that be?

VIKTOR. A worm. Therein lies his power, comrades. An eternally laboring worm. A worm will crawl out and begin to gnaw away.

PUGACHYOV. Gnaw away at what?

VIKTOR. Let it begin with the weakest link. Do you happen to know Fedya Petunin?

ARISTARKH. Who is that?

VIKTOR. A marvelous type. A positive type. But with a touch of melancholy, comrades. We've got to drop a worm into him. One single worm. Do you know how quickly worms multiply?

SCENE TWENTY-THREE

(Enter Semyon)

SEMYON. You here to see me?

ARISTARKH. These people have learned of your splendid decision, citizen Podsekalnikov, and they have come to express to you their enthusiasm.

PUGACHYOV. You are our last hope, Semyon Semyonovich.

YELPIDY. You are a saint. A martyr.

VIKTOR. You are a hero.

RAISA. You are my most favorite contemporary hero.

SEMYON. Really now...

RAISA. Don't be modest. You really are a hero.

ARISTARKH. When have you decided to shoot yourself, Semyon Semyonovich?

SEMYON. I still haven't decided.

RAISA. Goodness gracious, don't be modest about it.

ARISTARKH. Shall we say, tomorrow at noon. Does that suit you?

SEMYON. Tomorrow?

ARISTARKH. Put it off 'til tomorrow, Semyon Semyonovich.

YELPIDY. We'll arrange a farewell party for you.

PUGACHYOV. We'll throw you a banquet, Semyon Semyonovich.

VIKTOR. We shall honor you, citizen Podsekalnikov.

ARISTARKH. Does tomorrow at ten suit you?

SEMYON. Tomorrow at ten?

ARISTARKH. The banquet.

SEMYON. Ah, the banquet... Yes, that's fine.

ARISTARKH. So, here's the arrangement: The farewell party starts at ten, and at twelve sharp you set off on your journey.

SEMYON. Journey? Where to?

ARISTARKH. I can't say. Nowhere... the unknown. We'll have to wait and see.

SEMYON. But, dear comrades, I don't know how to get there.

ARISTARKH. We'll come pick you up, Semyon Semyonovich. 'Til tomorrow, then. (*All leave except Semyon*)

SCENE TWENTY-FOUR

SEMYON. (*Alone*) So it's tomorrow I go. I've got to collect my things. My cigarette case... I'll give that to my brother in, uh, Yelets. My, uh, coat... the light one... I'll give that to my brother, too. And my striped pants... no, I'd better keep my pants for the banquet. Striped pants look good at banquets.

SCENE TWENTY-FIVE

(*Serafima and Mariya*)

MARIYA. Whoo! We're all out of breath. We barely caught Yegor Timofeyevich.

SEMYON. Iron my pants and patch the hole. I'll be wearing them tomorrow, Serafima Ilinishna.

SERAFIMA. Why wear out your good ones? Where are you going, Semyon Semyonovich?

SEMYON. To, uh, I, uh, found an... occupation.

MARIYA. Senya! That's marvelous! When?

SEMYON. Tomorrow at noon sharp.

MARIYA. Finally! What kind of a position is it? Temporary?

SEMYON. No, I would guess more or less permanent.

MARIYA. Mama, set up the iron. We'll iron and patch his pants right now.

(*Mariya and Serafima run out with the pants*)

SCENE TWENTY-SIX

SEMYON. *(Alone)* Tomorrow at noon sharp. If it happens at noon sharp, where will I be at half past twelve? Or even at five past? Where? Who can answer that question for me? Who?

SCENE TWENTY-SEVEN

(Enter an old woman and a young boy. The boy is carrying a small chest and a bundle)

OLD WOMAN. Can he sit here a moment?
SEMYON. Who?
OLD WOMAN. Anisya's nephew came to visit her. But Anisya's door is locked. If he could sit here a minute, I'll go run find his aunt. He won't bother you, Semyon Semyonovich. He's a quiet little thing. From the provinces.
SEMYON. Sure, leave him with me.

(The old woman leaves. The boy sits down)

SCENE TWENTY-EIGHT

(Semyon and the boy. A pause)

SEMYON. What do you think, young man? Only for God's sake, don't interrupt me. Just think about it for a minute first. Imagine that tomorrow at noon you take a revolver in your hand. For God's sake don't interrupt me. All right. Let's say you pick it up... and you put the barrel in your mouth. Wait a minute, you put the barrel in your mouth. All right, let's say you put it in your mouth. Like this. There, you've put it in your mouth. And the instant you put it in your mouth a second passes. Now, let's approach this second philosophically. What is a second? Tick-tock. Yeah. Tick-tock. And between the tick and the tock there's a wall. That's right, a wall. That is, the barrel of the revolver. You see what I'm driving at? So here's the barrel of the gun. Here's tick. Here's tock. And tick, young man, is everything you ever knew, while tock, young man, is already nothing. No-thing. You understand me? Why? Because here you've got the trigger. Now, let's approach a trigger philosophically. You approach it, and now you're at it. You squeeze it. Wham! Bang! And wham, that's still tick, but bang, well, that's already tock. Now, I understand everything that concerns tick and wham, but I understand absolutely nothing about tock and bang. Tick—

123

and I'm still here with myself, my wife, my mother-in-law, the sun, the air and the water—I understand all of that. But tock—and now I've got no wife... although I can understand having no wife... and I've got no mother-in-law... although I have no trouble whatsoever imagining no mother-in-law... but me without me, that's entirely beyond me. How can I be without me? Do you understand? Me. Me personally. Podsekalnikov. A hu-man-be-ing. Now, let's approach a human being philosophically. Darwin proved to us in the language of pure mathematics that a human being is a cage. For God's sake, don't interrupt me. A man is a cage. And in this cage there languishes a soul. That I understand. But you shoot, and you break open the cage, and the soul comes flying out of it. It flies out. It flies around. Well, of course, it flies around crying, "Hosanna! Hosanna!" And, of course, God calls it to Him. And God asks, "Whose soul are you?" "Podsekalnikov's." "Did you suffer?" "I suffered." "Well, go on then and dance." And the soul begins to sing and dance. *(Sings)* "Be there glory to mighty God, peace on earth, and good will among men." I understand all that. But what if the cage is empty? What if there is no soul? What then? What do you do then? What do you think? Is there life after death or not? *(Shakes the Boy)* I'm asking you, is there or not? Is there or not? Answer me. Answer.

(Enter the old woman)

SCENE TWENTY-NINE

(Semyon, the old woman and the boy)

OLD WOMAN. Thank you Semyon Semyonovich. I found the key. Poor boy here's a deaf-mute, you know. Can't say a thing. Thank you, thank you.

(They leave)

SEMYON. So then it's tomorrow at noon.

END OF ACT II

ACT III

(An outdoor restaurant, "The Red Beau-Monde," in a summer garden. At table are Alexander, Aristarkh, Pugachyov, Viktor, Father Yelpidy, Stepan Vasilyevich Peresvetov, Margarita, Cleopatra, Raisa, Zinka Padespan and Grunya. There is a Gypsy choir on a platform beside the shooting gallery. The Gypsies sing a toast to Podsekalnikov's health. Semyon is draped with streamers and covered with confetti)

SCENE ONE

GYPSIES. *(Sing)*
>Our dear Semyon Semyonovich
>Has come to visit us.
>Senya, Senya, Senya,
>Senya, Senya, Senya.
>Senya, Senya, drink it all up.
>Senya, Senya, drink it all up.

(A gypsy woman gives Semyon a glass of wine on the back of her guitar. All applaud)

Drink it all up, drink it all up, drink it all up, drink it all up.

(Semyon drinks the wine, then smashes down the glass. The guests applaud)

PUGACHYOV. There's a real hussar for you! A real daredevil! Now that's the way to do it!
MARGARITA. That's what I love you for, Semyon Semyonovich. Kostya! Kostenka! Kostka, damn it!

(A waiter comes running)

Mark down ninety kopecks for the glass. Drink! Drink! What's the matter, Semyon Semyonovich?
SEMYON. What time is it, huh?
MARGARITA. It's a long time 'til noon, Semyon Semyonovich.
SEMYON. A long time?
MARGARITA. A long time, Semyon Semyonovich. Don't think, drink,

125

Semyon Semyonovich.

YELPIDY. *(Leans toward Grunya)* Pushkin once went to the bathhouse...

GRUNYA. Don't you dare tell any Pushkin stories. I don't like pornography.

SEMYON. Waiter!

SECOND WAITER. Yes, sir?

SEMYON. What time is it, huh?

SECOND WAITER. It should soon be noon, Semyon Semyonovich.

SEMYON. Soon?

SECOND WAITER. Soon, Semyon Semyonovich.

YELPIDY. *(Leans toward Raisa)* Pushkin once went to the bathhouse...

(Raisa begins to whinny like a horse)

RAISA. *(Whinnying)* Oh, you naughty man! I can't stand it! I can picture it all so clearly! And then?...

YELPIDY. So, Pushkin came to the bathhouse...

ARISTARKH. Respected guests! We have gathered to bid farewell to Semyon Semyonovich as he departs, if I can express it so, for a better world. To a world from which no one returns.

STEPAN VASILYEVICH. Ah, he must be going abroad.

PUGACHYOV. No, a bit farther, Stepan Vasilyevich.

STEPAN VASILYEVICH. I bid you a pleasant journey.

ARISTARKH. Stop interrupting me, citizen.

VOICES. Quiet! Quiet!

(A deathly silence falls)

YELPIDY. So then Pushkin takes off his pants...

(Raisa starts to whinny)

VOICES. Quiet! Quiet! *(All fall deathly silent)*

YELPIDY. So, Pushkin starts taking off his underwear.

VOICES. Quiet! Quiet!

RAISA. *(Whinnying)* I can imagine it all so clearly... And then?...

ARISTARKH. Dearly beloved Semyon Semyonovich. You have chosen a splendid and righteous path. Go your way with confidence and conviction, that others may follow you.

RAISA. *(Whinnying)* And the bathhouse attendant, what did she do?

ARISTARKH. Many rebellious, excitable, and youthful heads shall be turned toward the path you blaze. And many fathers shall weep over them, many mothers shall wail beside their graves, and finally the great motherland shall shudder, and the great gates of the Kremlin shall swing open wide and our leaders will come out to meet us. Our leading leader shall extend a hand to the merchant, the merchant shall extend a hand to the laborer, the laborer shall extend a hand to the factory worker, the factory worker shall extend a hand to the peasant, the peasant shall extend a hand to the landowner, the landowner shall extend a hand to his estate, his estate shall extend... ah! who wouldn't be satisfied on an estate that extends so far and wide?

YELPIDY. So Pushkin goes for her... you know, it rhymes with "mass."

ARISTARKH. Fame and glory to you, beloved Semyon Semyonovich. Hurrah!

ALL. Hur-r-r-rah.

SEMYON. Dear guests.

VOICES. Shhhh....

ALEXANDER. May we have silence and attention.

(A deathly silence falls)

You now may speak, Semyon Semyonovich.

SEMYON. What time is it, huh?

MARGARITA. Don't think, drink, Semyon Semyonovich.

PUGACHYOV. I'm not much of a critic, Aristarkh Dominikovich, I'm a butcher. But I've got to say, Aristarkh Dominikovich, that you spoke marvelously. I think it would be a wonderful thing, Aristarkh Dominikovich, for our government to extend a hand.

ARISTARKH. I think it would be even more wonderful if our government would turn up its toes and fall flat on its...

PUGACHYOV. Let's be satisfied with a hand, for the time being, Aristarkh Dominikovich.

STEPAN VASILYEVICH. I hope you'll pardon me. I wasn't aware that you are shooting yourself at noon today. Allow me to toast your health.

SEMYON. What time is it now?

MARGARITA. Don't think, drink, Semyon Semyonovich.

ZINKA PADESPAN. Gentlemen, show a little style. Let's liven things up.

YELPIDY. I suggest that we shout "hurrah!"

VIKTOR. Everyone!

ALL. Hur-r-r-rah.

ALEXANDER. Waiters! Champagne!

PUGACHYOV. Music! For ten rubles sing us something about the soul.

GYPSIES.

> Mama, mama, life is so tedious,
> Oh, darling mine, life is so sad.

YELPIDY. There we go!

ALEXANDER. Pick it up!

VIKTOR. Move it! Move it!

YELPIDY. You know, there's something in that.

PUGACHYOV. My dear friends, I am truly touched.

ARISTARKH. I didn't weep when my own mother passed away! My own poor mother, dear comrades. But now... But now... (Weeps)

RAISA. I just saw it all so clearly—dictatorship, the republic, the revolution... Won't somebody tell me, who needs it all?

VIKTOR. What do you mean, who? Is that the way to ask such a question? I can't imagine myself without the Soviet republic. I agree with almost everything that is happening in it. I only want just a tiny bit more. Wrapped in a fur coat, flying across the steppes in a wide-runner sledge, beneath the tinkling of bells in the bright morning light with my grey beaver hat cocked back on my head and surrounded by Gypsies, with my beloved dog clutched in my arms, I want to count out the versts[1] of my unfortunate homeland. I want the guitar strings to burst, the coachman to weep in his homespun mittens, I want to cast off my hat, I want to plunge into a snowdrift and pray, to swear an oath, to blaspheme, to repent, and then to down in a gulp an icy mug of beer, I want to whistle, to sigh at the whole of the universe and to fly... And I want to do it our way, the Russian way, so that my soul is ripped out and cast to the devil, so that the earth reels beneath my sledge's runners like a child's spinning top, so that my horses fly over the earth like birds on the wing. O, horses, my horses, what horses! And my troika is no longer a troika, but Russia herself, and she races onward, inspired by God. Russia, where are you racing to? Give me your answer.

SCENE TWO

(Enter Yegor)

YEGOR. Straight to the police, mark my word.

VIKTOR. What do you mean, the police? What for?

YEGOR. Because you can't drive like that. You can drive only as fast as the law provides, no faster than fifty versts per hour.

VIKTOR. But that was a metaphor, inspiration.

YEGOR. Let me offer you some advice. Have your inspirations within the bounds of the law. So tell, me, is the shooting gallery open or not?

ALEXANDER. We've been waiting for you, Yegor Timofeyevich. We'd almost given up on your coming.

MARGARITA. Have a little nip, Yegor Timofeyevich.

---

[1] A Russian measurement of distance roughly equivalent to two-thirds of a mile.

YEGOR. I don't drink.

ALEXANDER. Why don't you drink, Yegor Timofeyevich?

YEGOR. I'm afraid of getting used to it.

ALEXANDER. What's there to fear? Here, try some.

YEGOR. No, I'm afraid to.

ALEXANDER. What are you afraid of, Yegor Timofeyevich?

YEGOR. What do you mean, what? It might happen that no sooner do you get used to it, than—wham!—socialism comes along, and there's no wine under socialism. Then what are you going to do when you want to get your hands on a drink?

MARGARITA. Just one little glass, one little glass. For the ladies.

YEGOR. By the way, there will be no ladies under socialism, either.

PUGACHYOV. What nonsense! Humans can't live without ladies.

YEGOR. And by the way, there won't be any humans under socialism, either.

VIKTOR. What do you mean? What will there be, then?

YEGOR. Masses, masses, and masses. An enormous mass of masses.

ALEXANDER. So then, drink to the masses.

YEGOR. Well, I can't refuse the masses.

PUGACHYOV. Pour the drinks.

YELPIDY. Make 'em strong.

ALEXANDER. Down the hatch.

GYPSIES. (Sing)

> Our dear friend Yegor Timofeyevich
> Has come to visit us.
> Georgie, Georgie, Georgie,
> Georgie, Georgie, Georgie,
> Georgie, Georgie, drink it up,
> Georgie, drink it up.

ALEXANDER. So, how is it?

YEGOR. Not bad. I love it when people sing songs about me, although nowadays people usually go in for all kinds of nonsense.

VIKTOR. Who for instance?

YEGOR. Take you for instance. You're a writer, what do you write about?

VIKTOR. About everything.

YEGOR. There's one for you. About everything. Tolstoy wrote about everything, too. That doesn't interest us. I'm a courier and I want to read about couriers. You understand that?

VIKTOR. But I've written about foundry workers.

YEGOR. Well then let the foundry workers read you. But foundry workers don't interest couriers. I repeat, I'm a courier and I want to read about couriers. Understand? What do you think about that?

SEMYON. Yegor, what do you think, is there life after death or not?

129

YEGOR. At present, there may be, but there won't be under socialism. I can
guarantee that.
MARGARITA. Where are you going? Come here, have a seat.
CLEOPATRA. Make my acquaintance. Cleopatra Maximovna.
RAISA. *(To her neighbor at the table)* Oleg Leonidovich told me straight out, "I
can't get your splendid stomach out of my head."
ALEXANDER. To the health of the masses, Yegor Timofeyevich!
YEGOR. I can't refuse. I always stand ready to serve.
MARGARITA. Don't eat, Semyon Semyonovich, drink.
YELPIDY. Let's drink to the ladies.
ZINKA PADESPAN. Merci, good father.
CLEOPATRA. You haven't seen life, Yegor Timofeyevich. There's a whole
other beautiful, miraculous life. Life with linens, fine furniture, furs,
cosmetics. Admit it, Yegor Timofeyevich, haven't you ever been tempted to
see the sights of, say, Paris?
YEGOR. I admit it's true, Cleopatra Maximovna. I even began saving up my
money.
CLEOPATRA. For the trip you mean.
YEGOR. For a tower, Cleopatra Maximovna.
CLEOPATRA. For what tower?
YEGOR. For a very tall one.
CLEOPATRA. What do you need with a tower, Yegor Timofeyevich?
YEGOR. What do you mean? Imagine that I've already built a tower. And the
instant I have a desire to take a peek at Paris, I simply climb up in my tower
and take a good, long look, Cleopatra Maximovna. From a Marxist point of
view.
CLEOPATRA. And?
YEGOR. Well, and who would want to live in such a Paris?
CLEOPATRA. Why's that?
YEGOR. You will never understand me, Cleopatra Maximovna. You're a
woman of a different class.
ARISTARKH. Pardon me, but what other class? If I may inquire, Yegor
Timofeyevich, who do you think made the revolution?
YEGOR. The revolution? Me. That is, us.
ARISTARKH. You oversimplify, Yegor Timofeyevich. Allow me to illustrate
my point with a little allegory.
YEGOR. I can't refuse. I always stand ready to serve.
ARISTARKH. An allegory, so to speak, from the menagerie of domestic
animal life.
ALL. Yes! Yes!
MARGARITA. Don't listen, Semyon Semyonovich, drink.
ARISTARKH. Once upon a time, some duck eggs were placed beneath a
good-hearted chicken. She sat on those eggs for years on end. For years she

warmed them with her warm body, and finally they hatched. The ducks pecked their way out of the eggs and, tumbling over one another in excitement, they crawled out from under the chicken. Then they grabbed her by the neck and dragged her to the river. "But I am your mother," cried the chicken. "I sat on you for years. What are you doing?" "Swim!" cried the ducks. Do you understand the allegory?

VOICES. Somehow, uh, not quite.

ARISTARKH. Who do you think this chicken is? It's our intelligentsia. And who were these eggs? These eggs are the proletariat. The intelligentsia sat on the proletariat for years on end. It sat, and sat, and sat, and finally sat itself out. The proletariat pecked its way out, grabbed the intelligentsia, and dragged it to the river. "I am your mother," cried the intelligentsia. "I sat on you for years. What are you doing?" "Swim!" cried the ducks. "I can't swim!" "Then fly!" "But a chicken is no bird!," cried the intelligentsia. "Then just sit there." And that's just what the intelligentsia has done ever since— under lock and key. Take my brother-in-law, for instance. He's been in prison five years. Now do you get the allegory?

ZINKA PADESPAN. What's there to understand? He probably made off with government money.

ARISTARKH. The money was a minor detail. But tell me, why did we hatch those eggs? If we had known then what we know now, we could have used those eggs for... What would you have used them for, citizen Podsekalnikov?

SEMYON. Egg-nog.

ARISTARKH. You're a genius, Semyon Semyonovich. Those are golden words.

GRUNYA. Why the long face, citizen Podsekalnikov?

SEMYON. Tell me, dear comrades, can you understand the most important thing? And if you can, then tell me, dear comrades, is there life after death or not?

ALEXANDER. You'd better ask the priest about that one. That's his specialty.

YELPIDY. How would you like me to answer, according to religion or according to conscience?

SEMYON. Is there a difference?

YELPIDY. E-nor-mous. Or, I can even give you an answer according to science.

SEMYON. Just tell me the truth, Father.

YELPIDY. Religion says yes, science says no, and conscience says no one has the foggiest notion.

SEMYON. No one? Then there's not even any point in asking?

YELPIDY. What's the problem, you silly man? You'll find out yourself in half an hour.

SEMYON. A half an hour? You mean it's eleven thirty? How? Eleven thirty?

MARGARITA. Don't think, Semyon Semyonovich, drink.

SEMYON. Is it really eleven thirty? Eleven thir... Sing the service, dear comrades. Sing, my beloveds. Sing, you bastards.

(The Gypsies bellow out a song)

I'll suffer for everyone. I'll suffer for everyone.

GYPSIES. Sing it again! Sing it again!

SEMYON. There's where life begins, comrades. Life begins thirty minutes before death.

YEGOR. To the health of the masses!

GYPSIES. Sing it again! Sing it again!

SEMYON. The masses! Listen to Semyon Podsekalnikov! Right now I am dying. And who is to blame? The leaders are to blame, dear comrades. Go straight up to any leader and ask him, "What have you done for Podsekalnikov?" He won't give you an answer, comrades, because he doesn't even know that there is a Podsekalnikov in the Soviet Republic. But there is a Podsekalnikov, dear comrades. And I am him. You can't see me from there, comrades. But you just wait. I'll rise to such grandiose proportions that you'll be able to see me from anywhere in the land. If I can't get what's owed me in life, I'll get it in death. I'll die, and when I'm dead and buried I'll begin to speak. I'll speak out bravely and openly for everyone. I'll tell them that I am dying for... for... that I am dying for... for... Dammit! How the hell can I tell them what I'm dying for, comrades, when I haven't even read my own suicide note?

ARISTARKH. We'll settle everything right now, Semyon Semyonovich. Margarita Ivanovna, bring us a table and chair.

MARGARITA. Kostya! A table!

(The waiters carry in a table and chair. On the table is a pen, paper, a vase with flowers, a bottle of champagne, and a work light with a green lamp shade)

ARISTARKH. Be so kind as to read this, citizen Podsekalnikov.

SEMYON. What is it?

ARISTARKH. It's all written right here.

SEMYON. "Why I can't go on living!" That's it, that's it. I've wanted to know this for a long time.

ARISTARKH. Just sit down and copy it out.

(Semyon takes a seat at the table)

We won't bother you, Semyon Semyonovich. Be so kind, maestro, a quiet waltz.

(Music)

SEMYON. *(Copying)* "Why I can't go on living!" Exclamation point. And then, "Humans and Communists, gaze into the eyes of history." Oh, how it's written here, huh? "Gaze into the eyes of history." Marvelous. Beautiful.

PUGACHYOV. Respected friends. I love beauty so much it's terrifying. Beauty, my respected friends...

ZINKA PADESPAN. Nikifor, you're going to vomit. I assure you.

PUGACHYOV. Who, me? Be my guest. As much as you like.

SEMYON. *(Reads)* "Because the cleansing frenzy of the revolution has touched us all!" Exclamation point. Underlined. *(Copies)*

CLEOPATRA. This miserable, dull life disgusts me. I long for dissonance, Yegor Timofeyevich.

YEGOR. Waiter!

KOSTYA. Yes, sir?

YEGOR. Dissonances. And bring two of 'em. One for me and one for the lady.

KOSTYA. Right away, sir.

SEMYON. *(Reads)* "Don't forget that the intelligentsia is the salt of the earth, and should it pass into oblivion, you will have nothing left to season the porridge you've cooked up." Got it: "Don't forget..." *(Copies)*

VIKTOR. The worm has emerged, Aristarkh Dominikovich.

ARISTARKH. What are you talking about?

VIKTOR. Yesterday I told you about Fedya Petunin. A marvelous type, a positive type, but the worm is already gnawing him, Aristarkh Dominikovich.

RAISA. They tell me you've been abroad.

VIKTOR. I've been to the working neighborhoods of France.

RAISA. Tell me, what size breasts are the Parisian women wearing this year in France, small or large?

VIKTOR. Each according to her own means.

CLEOPATRA. That's just as I would have expected. Ah, Paris... And here? Even a woman of means has to stay as she is.

SEMYON. "The intelligentsia needs its freedom."

PUGACHYOV. I need a bath! I need a bath! Margarita Ivanovna, I need a bath!

MARGARITA. What for?

PUGACHYOV. I want to go for a swim with a couple of these floozies.

SEMYON. Exclamation point. That, comrades, is what I'm dying for. Signature.

(Pugachyov begins to weep)

ZINKA PADESPAN. What's the matter, Nikifor Arsentyevich?
PUGACHYOV. I feel sick. I'm sick with nostalgia for my homeland.
ARISTARKH. What homeland? Where are you from?
PUGACHYOV. Russia, my dear comrades.
SEMYON. Beloved citizens, do you realize...?
VOICES. What's he up to, now?
SEMYON. Wait a minute. Do you realize what I can do? Do you realize what I can do? I don't have to fear anyone, comrades. No one at all. Whatever I want to do, I can do it. I'm going to die anyway. I'm dying anyway. Do you see? Whatever I want to do, I can do. My God! I can do anything. My God! I fear no one. For the first time in my life I fear no one. If I want to, I can go to any meeting—note that I say *any* meeting, comrades—and I can stick my tongue out at the chairman. You think I can't? I can, dear comrades. That's the whole point, that I can do anything. Fearing no one. There are 140 million people in the Soviet Union, comrades, and each million is afraid of someone, but not me. I fear no one. No one. I'm going to die anyway. I'm dying anyway. Hold me down or I might start dancing. Today I rule over all people. I am a dictator. I am a tsar, dear comrades. I can do anything. Whatever I want to do, I can do it. What should I do? What should I do with this insane power, comrades? I want to do something for all mankind. I know. I know. I've got it. This is divine, citizens. Comrades, right now, I am going to telephone the Kremlin. The Kremlin. The red heart of the Soviet Republic. I'll call them... and I'll... I'll... I'll chew somebody out. What do you say to that? Huh? *(Goes to the phone)*
ARISTARKH. For God's sake!
CLEOPATRA. No, don't, Semyon Semyonovich.
YELPIDY. What are you doing?
MARGARITA. Help!
SEMYON. Shush! *(Picks up the receiver)* All are silent when a giant speaks with a giant. Give me the Kremlin. That's all right, sweetheart, no need to fear. Just give me the Kremlin. Who is this? The Kremlin? Podsekalnikov speaking. Pod-se-kal-ni-kov. An individual. An in-di-vi-du-al. Give me somebody there. I don't care, give me the biggest one you've got. He's not there? Well, then tell him for me that I read Marx and I didn't like him. Shut up! Don't interrupt me. And then you can tell him, that they can all go to... Hello? Hello? My God. *(Drops the receiver in shock)*
ARISTARKH. What happened?
SEMYON. They hung...
VIKTOR. What?
YELPIDY. Who did they hang?
SEMYON. The receiver. They hung up the receiver. I scared them. They were

frightened of me. Do you see that? Do you grasp the situation? The Kremlin was afraid of me. What am I, comrades? It's frightening even to analyze it. Just think about it. From my earliest childhood I wanted to be a genius, but my parents were against it. What have I lived for? For what? To be a statistic. Life mine, how many years have you made a fool of me? How many years have you humiliated me? But today my hour has come. Life, I demand satisfaction.

(The clock chimes twelve. Deathly silence)

MARGARITA. You'd best be off, Semyon Semyonovich.
SEMYON. What, already? Isn't your clock a bit fast, Margarita Ivanovna?
MARGARITA. No, we're synchronized with the post office, Semyon Semyonovich.

(Pause)

ALEXANDER. Well, let's all sit a moment for good luck.

(All sit. Pause)

SEMYON. Well, farewell, comrades. *(Goes toward the exit. Returns, takes the bottle of champagne and slips it into his pocket)* Forgive me... I'll just take this for courage. *(Goes toward exit)*
KOSTYA. Come visit us again, Semyon Semyonovich.
SEMYON. No, next time it's your turn to come see me. *(Leaves)*

END OF ACT III

ACT IV

(A room in Podsekalnikov's apartment)

SCENE ONE

(Serafima is mixing up some egg nog)

SERAFIMA. *(Sings)*
>   The storm howled,
>   The rain poured,
>   In the darkness, lightning flashed.
>   And the thunder thundered endlessly,
>   And in the darkness raged a storm.

SERAFIMA and MARIYA. *(From the other room)*
>   And the thunder thundered endlessly,
>   And in the darkness raged a storm.

SERAFIMA. *(Sings)* "Sleep ye little ones..."
MARIYA. *(From the other room)* Mama? Mama?
SERAFIMA. What do you want, Masha?

SCENE TWO

(Mariya holds a kerosene lamp, out of which are protruding curling tongs)

MARIYA. What do you think Senya would like better, big or small curls?
SERAFIMA. Who knows, Masha?
MARIYA. But what should I do?
SERAFIMA. I think what you should do, Masha, is to make small ones in front and big ones in back. That way you can't miss. *(Sings)* "Sleep ye little ones..."
MARIYA. He'll probably be back soon, Mama. You'd better start beating faster.
SERAFIMA. I'm working as fast as I can. I've already whipped up two measly yolks into a whole glass-full.
MARIYA. What a fanatic he is for egg-nog.
SERAFIMA. Well, he can indulge his sweet tooth, now. *(Sings)* "Sleep ye

136

young heroes, comrades in the storm..."

MARIYA. What do you think, mama, will he get the job or not?

SERAFIMA. How can you even ask? Of course he will.

MARIYA. If they tell him there's no work, it'll be the end of him.

SERAFIMA. How could there be no work in Russia? We've got more work than all mankind can handle. Just take a look around you.

MARIYA. Then, how come everybody doesn't have a job?

SERAFIMA. It's all a matter of connections.

MARIYA. How's that?

SERAFIMA. Because there's so much to be done in Russia that there aren't enough connections to go around. For example, let's say there's a job somewhere, but nobody has the right connections to get it. In that case, Masha, the job stays vacant. But if Senya's got connections, then you can bet he'll find work.

MARIYA. Do you really think we'll start a new life?

SERAFIMA. How can you doubt it?
(Sings)

> In the morning my voice shall ring out,
> Calling out to glory and death.

BOTH.

> In the morning my voice shall ring out,
> Calling out to glory and death.

MARIYA. Whose letter is this?

SERAFIMA. Oh, just throw it away. It's probably something old.

MARIYA. No it isn't. It's sealed and addressed to you.

SERAFIMA. Well then, read it to me, Masha.

MARIYA. What? *(Reads)* "Respected Serafima Ilinishna. By the time you read this letter, I shall no longer be among the living. Please break the news to Masha gently."

SERAFIMA. Merciful heavens!

MARIYA. Wait a minute. *(Reads)* "Send my light coat and cigarette case to my brother in Yelets. Signed, Semyon." How can this be? What does it mean? Oh, Lord! *(Falls on the bed weeping)*

SERAFIMA. Masha! Masha! Don't weep, for God's sake, don't weep.

SCENE THREE

(The door flies open. Enter Aristarkh, Father Yelpidy, Alexander, a hatmaker, a seamstress and Margarita)

YELPIDY. Weep, widow Podsekalnikov, weep. Embrace your children and raise your voice in lament, "Where is your father? Your father is no more. Your father is no more and shall never be again."

ALEXANDER. He never was.

YELPIDY. What?

ALEXANDER. There was no father, I tell you.

YELPIDY. Why?

ALEXANDER. Because there weren't any children.

YELPIDY. Oh? There's a good one for you. Oh well, nothing he can do about it now. He missed his chance. So, he wasn't a father. Weep, widow Podsekalnikov, weep.

ARISTARKH. Let's leave that 'til later, shall we, father? Allow me to speak. Dear Mariya Lukyanovna, allow me to address you with a small request in the name of the Russian intelligentsia. Your husband has perished, but his corpse is full of life. He lives in our midst as a social truth. Let us support his new life together. I relinquish the floor. And now, Henrietta Stepanovna, attend to your duties, if you will.

HATMAKER. Pardon me, madame. Does madame desire a straw hat or a panama? Or perhaps she would prefer a felt hat. This would certainly be elegant head wear for a funeral.

MARIYA. I don't want anything... what for?... Oh my God...

MARGARITA. Now, now, Mariya Lukyanovna, don't be like that. The funeral will be quite stylish. Why should you look worse than everyone else?

SERAFIMA. How is it going to be stylish, Margarita Ivanovna? We have nothing to bury him with.

ALEXANDER. Don't you worry about that, Serafima Ilinishna. These people are providing an unlimited expense account for everything from the burial to the sewing of your mourning attire.

SEAMSTRESS. Shall we begin with the measurements, madame?

MARIYA. Comrades... I can't... please leave me alone...

ARISTARKH. There's no need for widow's tears. Your husband died a hero. What is there to weep about?

MARIYA. But how am I going to live?...

ARISTARKH. I'll tell you how, Mariya Lukyanovna. Live just as your husband died, for he died a death worth imitating.

SEAMSTRESS. *(Measuring)* Length in front: forty-one.

ARISTARKH. Alone, absolutely alone, and with pistol in hand, he set off down the great road of Russian history.

SEAMSTRESS. *(Measuring)* Length in back: ninety-four.

ARISTARKH. There he fell and there he now lies...

SERAFIMA. Where?

ALEXANDER. On the road of history, Serafima Ilinishna.

SERAFIMA. Where's that? Someplace outside the city, I imagine?

ALEXANDER. Somewhat further.

ARISTARKH. He lies there as a terrible and universal stumbling block.

SEAMSTRESS. Perhaps you'd like to liven things up with lace?

ARISTARKH. May he, who travels that road today, Mariya Lukyanovna, stumble on Podsekalnikov's corpse.

HATMAKER. Now here is a splendid hat. It's called "fantasy cut." We can also do it in crepe, with a little bell on the rim.

ARISTARKH. And when this man stumbles, Mariya Lukyanovna, naturally he will look beneath his feet. And when he looks beneath his feet, naturally he will see us. And we shall say to him...

HATMAKER. Shall we try it on, madame?

ARISTARKH. You, who are traversing the road of history—you begetters of nations, you builders of life—look ye carefully unto the corpse of Podsekalnikov.

SERAFIMA. Careful, now.

MARGARITA. And now to the side.

HATMAKER. Voila. Divine.

ARISTARKH. And when he looks, he shall ask us, "What does this mean, this corpse of Podsekalnikov?" And we shall say to him, "This is our response to what you have wrought."

DRESSMAKER. Now, would you care for pleats? Or would you prefer it flared at the bottom?

ARISTARKH. Yes, Mariya Lukyanovna, your husband died a hero.

MARIYA. Would it be possible to have flared pleats?

ARISTARKH. Honor and glory to the widow Podsekalnikov! Honor and glory to the wife of the dear departed!

SERAFIMA. Where is he, by the way?

ARISTARKH. You'll have to ask the police about that. We shall be leaving you now, Mariya Lukyanovna, but we'll be right back. We shall not abandon you in your hour of misfortune. I didn't weep when my own mother passed away, my own poor mother, Mariya Lukyanovna, but now... now... Allow me to kiss you in the name of all those present. *(Kisses her)*

ALEXANDER. Allow me, too.

MARGARITA. Alexander! *(All exit except Serafima and Mariya)*

SCENE FOUR

(Mariya and Serafima)

SERAFIMA. What nice people. You see, Masha, there are still good people in the world.

MARIYA. People, yes, mama. But there is no Semyon.

SERAFIMA. Oh beloved! Oh departed! When are they coming to measure your dress?

MARIYA. Today at three. At the dressmaker's. Here's her card.

SERAFIMA. "La boutique de Madame Sofie." Expensive, I bet.

MARIYA. Not cheap, that's for sure. You could tell by the way she kept flitting about.

SERAFIMA. You'd better take off that hat before you ruin it, Masha.

MARIYA. So what if I ruin it? I don't care about anything anymore, mama. How can I go on? What do I need with my cursed life if I've never known complete happiness even once? First I had Senya, but I had no hat. Now I've got a hat, but I've got no Senya. Dear Lord, why can't you give us everything at once?

(A knock at the door)

SERAFIMA. Who is it?

SCENE FIVE

(Two suspicious figures carry Semyon's lifeless body into the room)

MARIYA. Mama! Dear Lord!

SERAFIMA. Saints preserve us! Over here! Put him over here!

MARIYA. Senya, darling. Senya, what have you done?

FIRST MAN. Nothing you can do about it now. Fate's little joke.

SECOND MAN. Yeah, we showed up about 15 seconds too late.

SERAFIMA. You mean you saw it happen?

SECOND MAN. Every bit of it.

FIRST MAN. True, we didn't think much about it at first, but then he says, "Take me home, will you?" And you wouldn't believe it. We walked a few steps away, he disappeared behind a tree, stood there a minute, and then—boom! —he hit the deck like a rock off a table. We came running, of course, but it was too late by then. By the time we got there he was dead to the world.

SECOND MAN. You might say he was one with the spirits.

(Mariya weeps)

FIRST MAN. You think she's going to go on wailing like this for long?

SERAFIMA. God grant that she get over it in a year or two.

FIRST MAN. A year or two? No reason for us to wait around, then. Let's get out of here.

(The two men leave)

SCENE SIX

(Serafima, Mariya and Semyon's corpse)

MARIYA. Mama and I tried to save you, Semyon, but now you are dead.

SEMYON. Dead? Who's dead? I'm dead? Oh Lord, hold me!

MARIYA. and SERAFIMA. Help!

SEMYON. Hold me, hold me down! I'm flying, I'm flying! Hosanna! Hosanna!

MARIYA. Senya! Senya!

SERAFIMA. Semyon Semyonovich!

SEMYON. Whose voice is that?

MARIYA. It's me, Mariya.

SEMYON. Mariya? What Mariya? The Mariya who begat God's word? The Mother of God herself? Mother of God, it's not my fault.

MARIYA. What's the matter with you Senya? It's me, Mariya.

SEMYON. Mariya? I'm sorry, I didn't recognize you. Allow me to introduce myself, I am the soul of Podsekalnikov.

MARIYA. He's gone off his rocker, mama.

SERAFIMA. Where have you been, Semyon Semyonovich? What have you done?

SEMYON. I suffered.

SERAFIMA. What do you mean, you suffered?

SEMYON. Holy Father, please believe me. I have every right to enter the heavenly gates. Holy Father, ask me to, and I'll sing and dance for you. *(Sings)* "Glory be to God on high, peace on earth..."

SERAFIMA. What's the matter with you? Snap out of it.

SEMYON. Heavenly Father...

SERAFIMA. I am not your father, Semyon Semyonovich. I am your mother-in-law.

SEMYON. What?

SERAFIMA. Your mother-in-law, Semyon Semyonovich.

SEMYON. My mother-in-law? Well, what do you know. So when did you kick the bucket, Serafima Ilinishna?

MARIYA. He's delirious. He probably wounded himself somewhere. *(Leans over him)* Senya, darling, did you... Ahhh!

SERAFIMA. What's the matter?

MARIYA. Take a whiff.

SERAFIMA. Holy...! Whew...! Where did you tie one on this time, Semyon Semyonovich?

SEMYON. Holy cherub! Most glorious seraph! Tell me, where does one go to join the other angels?

MARIYA. There he goes, he's at it again.

141

SERAFIMA. Give me a jug. Douse him with water, Masha. Go on, be quick about it. Douse him.

SEMYON. Where am I?... Oh, my God... Which world is this? The next one or this?

SERAFIMA. This one, this one.

MARIYA. What are you up to, you bum? First you leave a note that you've gone off to shoot yourself, and then you go and get drunk instead. You son of a bitch. You nearly drove me out of my mind. Here I am, a poor weak thing, weeping and carrying on.

SEMYON. Wait a minute.

MARIYA. No, you wait a minute. Here I am, a poor weak thing, weeping and carrying on. Here I am, the inconsolable widow, and you, you aren't even dead, you're just drunk. What are you trying to do, send me to my grave? What's the matter with you? Speak up when you're spoken to!

SEMYON. Wait a minute.

MARIYA. Well?

SEMYON. What time is it?

MARIYA. What time is it, he asks. It's two o'clock.

SEMYON. Two o'clock. How did that happen? Oh my God! At noon, Masha, at noon, I was supposed to... Wait a minute. When did I come here?

SERAFIMA. You didn't come, Semyon Semyonovich, you were brought.

SEMYON. Who brought me?

SERAFIMA. Two rather obnoxious characters.

SEMYON. Two men... yeah... now I remember... or at least something... they sat down and we all... that's right, we emptied the bottle...

MARIYA. You bum. Guzzling straight from the bottle.

SEMYON. I did it for courage, Masha. For courage, Masha, I drank and I drank and I drank. And when it came to the last bottle I went behind this tree, and I thought—I'll drink off this last one and then I can do it. You know what? I drank up the last bottle, but I still couldn't do it.

MARIYA. You buffoon. What is it you want?

SEMYON. Has anybody been here yet?

SERAFIMA. I'll say. Quite a sophisticated bunch.

SEMYON. What did they do?

SERAFIMA. They talked pretty words and expressed their sympathy.

MARIYA. They gave us an expense account to bury you. "Your husband," they said, "has died a hero."

SERAFIMA. How will we ever face them now?

MARIYA. They're going to want all their money back.

SERAFIMA. They're probably sewing her mourning dress as we speak. And what a dressmaker—Madame Sofie. That'll cost you a pretty penny, Semyon Semyonovich.

MARIYA. If we're lucky, maybe they haven't started yet. Come on, mama, let's go see Sofie right now.

SEMYON. Wait a minute. All isn't lost yet. I can still shoot myself.

MARIYA. Knock it off, Semyon. Let's go see Sofie, mama.

SEMYON. I'll shoot myself. You'll see. I'll shoot myself.

SERAFIMA. Shoot yourself—don't make me laugh, Semyon Semyonovich.
You'd be better off boiling up some tea.

(Mariya and Serafima rush out)

SCENE SEVEN

(Semyon alone)

SEMYON. They didn't believe me. They didn't believe me. Even Masha
didn't believe me. All right. You'll regret this one but good, Masha. Where
is it? Here it is. *(Takes out the pistol)* I've got to do this instantly, without
thinking, right in the heart. Instantaneous death. *(Holds the pistol to his chest)*
Instantaneous death. Or, maybe not. Better yet in the mouth. In the mouth
it's more instantaneous. *(Sticks the pistol in his mouth. Takes it out)* I'll count
to three. *(Puts it in his mouth)* Ah... ooo... *(Takes it out)* Or, maybe not. Better
to count to a thousand. *(Puts it in his mouth)* Ah... ooo... eee... oh... ai... i... e-
e... aaa... ai... *(Takes it out)* No, if you're going to count, you've got do it in
the heart. *(Holds the pistol to his chest)* One, two, three, four, five, six, seven,
eight, nine... Only a coward counts to a thousand. You've got to do it
instantly, decisively... I'll count to a hundred, and—wham! No, better yet
to fifteen. That's it. *(Holds the pistol to his chest again)* One, two, three, four,
five, six, seven, eight, nine, ten, eleven, twelve, thirteen, fourteen... Or
maybe it would be better not to count at all, and to do it in the mouth. *(Sticks
the pistol in his mouth. Takes it out)* But if you do it in the mouth, where does
the bullet go? Right here, into your head. What a waste of a head. I mean,
your face is on your head, comrades. Better to do it in the heart. But first
you've got to feel around to find out where it beats the hardest. Here. It's
beating here. And it's beating over here. And here, too! My God, what a big
heart. It beats everywhere you touch. It's beating so hard it's going to burst!
My God, if I die of a heart attack, I'll never be able to shoot myself. I can't
die, I can't die. I've got to live, live, live, so that I can live to shoot myself.
I'll never make it. I'm getting faint. I'll just catch my breath. For just a
moment. Beat, damn you. Beat like hell. *(The pistol drops out of his hand, he
falls)* Too late. I'm dying. Lord what have you done?

SCENE EIGHT

(Two boys with enormous wreaths wrapped in paper)

FIRST BOY. Does the deceased live here?
SEMYON. Who?
FIRST BOY. I said, does the deceased live here or not?
SEMYON. Who are you? Where are you from?
SECOND BOY. We're from "Eternity."
SEMYON. What do you mean, from eternity?
SECOND BOY. The "Eternity" funeral parlor. Take these, please. *(Sets down the wreaths)*
SEMYON. What's this?

(The boys remove the wrapping)

(Semyon reads what is written on the ribbons) "Sleep peacefully, Semyon Podsekalnikov. You are a hero." *(Reads at the other end)* "Admirers of your death." *(Reads another)* "To my unforgettable Senya, son-in-law and martyr to the cause. Your terribly grieving mother-in-law."
FIRST BOY. Are these for you?
SEMYON. Yes, for me... that is, for us.
FIRST BOY. Sign here, please. *(Hands him the receipt book)* No, over here.
SEMYON. *(Reads)* "For the receipt of six funeral wreaths." *(Signs)*
BOTH BOYS. Good day. *(They leave)*

SCENE NINE

(Semyon straightens the ribbon on a wreath. The writing is in French)

SEMYON. *(Reads)* "Pour mon Simon." What? Pour what where? This isn't for me. *(Runs to the door)* Boys, wait! *(Pause)* Oh well. *(Goes to another wreath, reads)* "Don't tell me he's dead. He's alive! Your Raisa." Oh my God! She figured it out. The bitch figured it out. Where's my pistol? Now I'll do it. *(Raises the pistol)* You say he's alive? All right. Just look at the life he's living. Just you look. *(Holds the pistol to his temple)* Sleep peacefully, Semyon Semyonovich. You're a hero. You're a hero. You're a hero, Podsekalnikov. Sleep. *(Drops his hand)* I may be a hero, but I can't fall asleep. No way I can sleep, comrades. I'm probably too tired. Exhausted. I'll just sit a bit and rest. That's it. I'll sit down with the paper and rest. And then I can go about my business, rested and invigorated. *(Sits down. Picks up the paper and reads)* "Hot Spots around the World." Hot spots around the world. What a bunch of hot air all that is when compared with the problems of a single human

144

being. (*Turns the paper over. Reads*) "Chronicle of Events." "An eighteen year-old boy drank acid..." Now there's an international hot spot for you. (*Reads*) "An unidentified citizen was run over by a trolley car at the corner of Semyonovsky Street and Drum Lane. The unknown man's body was sent to the morgue at the Filatov Hospital." Now there's a lucky man if I ever heard of one! One minute he's walking along thinking about nothing at all, and then—pow!—he's gone. But me... I keep thinking and thinking and I can't do a damn thing. Probably because I keep thinking about it. Yeah, that's it. Now I've got it. You've simply got to get hold of yourself, put everything aside, forget everything, empty your mind entirely, get in the right mood, and then go at it like a run-away trolley car. That's it. Just imagine that everything is beautiful, wonderful, marvelous, and then you're going along as if you're not thinking a thing, and then maybe you even start to sing a little something. Yeah, that's it, you start singing some sort of song. (*Begins to sing*) "Mama kisses us in swaddling / And others kiss us, too. / But when we're grown the girls kiss us / And that isn't all they do." Damn! Can you hear that trombone wailing? I think the trolley car is picking up speed. (*Brings his outstretched hand holding the pistol closer to his head*) What a charming sound... (*Stops his hand*) What a charming... I can't do this. Damn, that sounds great. I can't do this. Listen to that... Damn... Dammit all! I can't do this!

VOICE BEHIND THE DOOR. Come on, pull! Pull harder!

SCENE TEN

(*Three men carry in a coffin*)

FIRST MAN. Pull it over there. Over there! Where the hell are you going? Put it on the table.

(*They put the coffin on the table*)

There. Done.

SEMYON. Thank you very much gentlemen.

FIRST MAN. So where is he?

SEMYON. Where's who?

FIRST MAN. Podsekalnikov. The one who croaked.

SEMYON. Right here.

FIRST MAN. Where?

SEMYON. That is, not here... He's not here yet, but he'll be here soon. He's expected any minute now.

FIRST MAN. You must feel bad for the guy.

SEMYON. Comrades, I can't even begin to tell you!

FIRST MAN. Yeah, I always feel bad for dead people, too. Some change for our trouble?
SEMYON. Of course, of course.
FIRST MAN. Well, good luck.

(The three men leave)

SCENE ELEVEN

(Semyon stands dead still for several moments, then he goes to the coffin. He walks around it, peers inside, puffs up the pillow, and arranges the wreaths around it. He takes the pistol from his pocket and places it to his temple. He drops his hand. Goes to the mirror, hangs a black ribbon across it. Pause)

SEMYON. For some reason scientists haven't figured out a way yet for a man to shoot himself without feeling it. For example, why can't you shoot yourself under chloroform? And they call themselves the benefactors of mankind. They're sons of bitches, that's what they are. Lord Almighty! Oh, thou who dost give life! Give me the strength to kill myself. Can't you see that I can't do it myself? Can't you see?...

SCENE TWELVE

(Mariya and Serafima enter the room at a run)

MARIYA. They're coming!
SEMYON. Who's coming?
MARIYA. Everybody's coming!

(Mariya and Serafima run out of the room)

SCENE THIRTEEN

(Semyon races around the room. A noisy crowd can be heard approaching)

SEMYON. My God! My God!

(Noise grows louder and nearer)

My God! *(He leaps on the table)* My God! *(Jumps into the coffin)*

(The noise grows closer)

I'll wait it out here, and when they leave I'll do it. I'll do it once and for all. (*Lies down in the coffin*)

SCENE FOURTEEN

(*Aristarkh, Pugachyov, Alexander, Margarita, Raisa, Father Yelpidy, Yegor, Zinka Padespan, Grunya, a Deacon and a church choir enter through the wide-open doors. All are in mourning, many carry flowers. Terrified, Mariya and Serafima—both with their backs to the audience—try their best to hold back the crowd with outstretched arms*)

MARIYA. Put yourself in his shoes. People don't want to die. They don't want to die. Whose fault is that, comrades?
ARISTARKH. Others are to blame, Mariya Lukyanovna, not us.
SERAFIMA. But we're not blaming you, dear comrades.
MARIYA. Comrades, have you thought about how all this affects me?
ARISTARKH. We'll take your husband's place for you, Mariya Lukyanovna. We'll all pitch in.
SEMYON. (*In the coffin*) That's all I needed.
MARIYA. He didn't know what he was up to. He'll tell you so himself. Senya, Se... (*Sees him in the coffin*) Ah!
ARISTARKH. A chair for the widow! Quick, Yegor Timofeyevich!
SERAFIMA. (*Runs to Mariya*) What's the matter? (*Sees Semyon in the coffin*) Holy saints.
PUGACHYOV. Get another one. The mother-in-law needs help, too.

(*Yegor brings two chairs. Several people bustle around mother and daughter. Others go over to the coffin*)

MARGARITA. He looks alive!
ZINKA PADESPAN. But look, his nose looks dead.
MARIYA. Ahhh! Let me go! Let me go to him! He isn't dead, he's only a little drunk. He'll sleep it off and be good as new, Yegor Timofeyevich.
YEGOR. Calm down, Mariya Lukyanovna. I fear not.
MARIYA. He's alive, he's alive, I tell you.
RAISA. Listen to her bellow!
GRUNYA. She's probably a bit touched in the head from it all.
ARISTARKH. Take her into the other room.
MARIYA. Senya! Senya!
SERAFIMA. Wake up, Semyon Semyonovich!
ZINKA PADESPAN. And tell them to take the old woman out of here, too.
ALEXANDER. Grab the old woman, too, Yegor Timofeyevich.
MARIYA. He's alive! He's alive!

(Yegor leads Mariya and Serafima into the next room)

SCENE FIFTEEN

GRUNYA. What is wrong with those women?

MARGARITA. Listen to her. She's really gone over the edge.

MARIYA'S VOICE. *(From the next room)* He's alive! He's alive!

RAISA. Listen to her suffer, the poor woman.

ALEXANDER. It's always like that at first, and then you get sick of it. I know, I just buried a wife myself. I couldn't sleep for nights on end. If you don't believe me, just ask Margarita Ivanovna.

MARGARITA. Alexander!

MARIYA'S VOICE. Senya! Senya! Wake up!

GRUNYA. Just listen to her carrying on.

ZINKA PADESPAN. Let's go take a look. This must be something to see.

(All the women run to the next room)

SCENE SIXTEEN

(Aristarkh, Alexander, Father Yelpidy, Pugachyov, Viktor)

ALEXANDER. Now! May I pose a rather indelicate question. When do you all plan to pay up?

PUGACHYOV. Pay up for what?

ALEXANDER. What do you mean, for what? For the corpse. The merchandise is delivered and I want cash on the barrel. The arithmetic is simple.

ARISTARKH. All you ever talk about is money, comrade Kalabushkin. Don't ideas mean anything to you?

ALEXANDER. A good idea is one that feeds you, Aristarkh Dominikovich.

ARISTARKH. Around here, the only idea that feeds is one that turns into a slogan. Let's turn this idea into a slogan and it'll feed you, comrade Kalabushkin.

VIKTOR. The battle for ideas is a battle for bread.

ALEXANDER. I'd rather have less ideas and more bread. Let's clear up our accounts, comrades.

ARISTARKH. Allow me to note, please, that you haven't fulfilled all your promises yet.

ALEXANDER. How's that?

ARISTARKH. Have you had copies made of the suicide note?

ALEXANDER. The typist is at work as we speak, Aristarkh Dominikovich.

ARISTARKH. Then, begin spreading the word. The shot has been fired, let it be heard by thousands.

YELPIDY. You're counting on a large response, are you?

ARISTARKH. I am, I am, Father Yelpidy, although I'm also a bit concerned. I must admit freely, dear comrades, that our specimen is hardly extraordinary. If in his place, for example, some significant social figure had shot himself—say a writer like Gorky or some commissar—that would have been better, dear comrades.

SEMYON. *(In the coffin)* I think that's a great idea.

VIKTOR. That's just where you're wrong. We don't need a corpse as such. What is much more important is the way we serve the corpse up. The secret is in how you present it, Aristarkh Dominikovich. Just yesterday I was chatting with Fedya Petunin. How, you may ask? I drew him my own personal portrait of Podsekalnikov. And my portrait made Fedya Petunin fall in love with him. And now that the real Podsekalnikov is dead, what can Petunin possibly say about my creation? Absolutely nothing, except that it's the spitting image of the original, Aristarkh Dominikovich. Death in itself means nothing. Death is not infectious, but the reasons for death are, and we are free to dream up any reasons we choose.

ARISTARKH. We've got to get people whispering, comrades. That is the main thing.

YELPIDY. We'll lay him out in the chapel for two or three days and arrange for a fitting farewell.

ARISTARKH. Excellent idea. *(To Alexander)* Go get us some torchbearers.

(Exit Alexander)

SCENE SEVENTEEN

(Father Yelpidy, Aristarkh, Pugachyov, Viktor, the Deacon, and members of the choir)

YELPIDY. Shall we begin?

DEACON. Please do, Father Yelpidy. Start the prayers.

PUGACHYOV. It looks like we're beginning.

SCENE EIGHTEEN

(The same plus Yegor, Mariya, Serafima, Grunya, Zinka Padespan, and Raisa)

YELPIDY. God is omnipotent, now and forever.

CHOIR. Amen.

149

MARIYA. What are you doing? How can you read the last rites over a living
    man? What are you doing?
DEACON. Let us all pray together.
MARIYA. What are you doing? Let go of me.
CHOIR. Lord, have mercy.
SERAFIMA. Help!
DEACON. Lord, we pray thee for the souls of the dear departed.
CHOIR. Lord, have mercy.

SCENE NINETEEN

(Several women and men peek in the door. Among them is the deaf-mute)

MARGARITA. You want to watch, too? Come in. Join us, comrades.

(All enter. The deaf-mute stands next to the coffin, lights a candle)

DEACON. Lord, we pray thee absolve the sins of thy humble servant, our
    dear, departed Simeon.
MARIYA. What are you doing?
CHOIR. Lord, have mercy.
MARIYA. Police!
DEACON. May the memory of the Lord's humble servant, Simeon, rest in
    eternal peace.
MARIYA. Police!
DEACON. The windows! Shut the windows. Quiet in here. Blessed are they
    who are remembered.
CHOIR. Lord, have mercy.
DEACON. Absolve him his sins...
ARISTARKH. Listen, father. Can't you speed it up a bit? The word of God is
    holy, Father Yelpidy, but taking into account the present company, I think
    we can cut out the non-essential stuff.
YELPIDY. That we can do, Aristarkh Dominikovich. *(Goes to the choir,
    whispers)*
CHOIR. Lord, have mercy.
MARIYA. He's alive!
SERAFIMA. Wake him up, comrades!
DEACON. Lord, grant that we be free of sorrows, anger, or need.
CHOIR. Lord, have mercy.
MARIYA. Why doesn't he wake up, mama?
YELPIDY. *(Running the words together)* For thou art the resurrection and the
    life of thy servant Simeon. Christ our Lord, we praise thee, thy Father and
    the Holy Ghost who art everlasting and everlasting shall be.

CHOIR. Amen.
MARIYA. Maybe he really is dead, mama.
CHOIR. May he rest in everlasting peace.
MARIYA. Ahhh! Help me! I'm fainting! Water!

(All run to Mariya, except the deaf-mute who didn't hear her and remains by the coffin. The Choir sings. All bustle around Mariya. The deaf-mute kneels down, holding a candle. He bows down to the ground. The Choir sings. Semyon, overcome with emotion, sits up and reaches into his pocket for a handkerchief. At this moment, the deaf-mute rises up from his knees and prepares to cross himself. He raises his head and sees the corpse sitting up in the coffin, wiping the tears from his eyes. The deaf-mute lets out a cry and falls on his back)

VOICES. What happened? Another one! (All rush to him)

SCENE TWENTY

(Enter Alexander and the torchbearers)

ARISTARKH. Carry him out. Get him out of here quick.

(The torchbearers lift the coffin, and carry it away. The Choir sings)

MARIYA. (Having come to) He's dead. He's dead.

(The deaf-mute rushes to her. Terrified, he tries to make her understand what he has seen by gesturing with his arms and hands. He takes out his handkerchief and wipes his eyes)

You sorry for him, too? Are you crying? I am so sad, I simply don't know what to do. (She embraces the deaf-mute)

(The Choir sings)

END OF ACT IV

ACT V

(A freshly-dug grave and mounds of dirt in a cemetery)

SCENE ONE

(Alexander, Aristarkh, Viktor)

ALEXANDER. Just look at it from over here, comrades. How do you like that?

ARISTARKH. I would say the location is quite nice.

ALEXANDER. As if you'd chosen it for yourself, Aristarkh Dominikovich.

ARISTARKH. By the way, I keep meaning to ask you. Have all the invitations been sent?

ALEXANDER. Every last one.

VIKTOR. No, not every one.

ARISTARKH. Why not?

VIKTOR. We completely forgot about Fedya Petunin. He should have got one, too.

ARISTARKH. Why didn't you give him one?

VIKTOR. Unfortunately, I haven't seen him for two days. I've been too busy, Aristarkh Dominikovich.

ARISTARKH. Well, that's not so important.

VIKTOR. What do you think is important?

ARISTARKH. Most important is for the public to catch wind of it.

SCENE TWO

(Two old women pass by the grave)

FIRST. What an old fool I am.

SECOND. What's the matter?

FIRST. Look here, another new grave. How could I have missed that?

SECOND. I saw it this morning. I was on my way to church and I saw it then.

FIRST. Well, who is it?

SECOND. One of our parish. Serafima Ilinishna's son-in-law, Podsekalnikov.

FIRST. How could I have missed that?

SECOND. He lay in the chapel two days. I went to see him yesterday with

Pankratyevna.

FIRST. You mean Pankratyevna saw him too?

SECOND. We both stood there and wept and wept.

FIRST. How could I have missed that? What happened to him?

SECOND. He did himself in, himself.

FIRST. How terrible. How could I have missed that? So, what did he do himself in for?

SECOND. What for? That's obvious.

FIRST. True, that's true. Oh, my, my. Dear, dear, dear.

(The two old women leave)

ARISTARKH. Did you see that? The public has finally caught wind of it. Come on, let's go.

(Alexander and Aristarkh leave)

SCENE THREE

(Two more old women pass by)

FIRST. Our cemetery is awfully depressing these days. It gives you the chills. It's not like the old days when people knew how to liven up a burial and all the corpses were interesting people.

SECOND. Nowadays corpses are no different from firewood. They just burn them and shovel them up in a jar.

FIRST. They burn them because they don't think about the future. And when the time comes for resurrection, there's nothing left to resurrect. My, my, my. But it's too late then.

SECOND. We'll have a good laugh on them then, won't we Pankratyevna?

(They leave)

SCENE FOUR

(Cleopatra rushes in, pulling Oleg Leonidovich by the arm)

CLEOPATRA. There.

OLEG. What?

CLEOPATRA. Here.

OLEG. Where?

CLEOPATRA. They're going to bury him here.

OLEG. Who are they going to bury?

CLEOPATRA. Oleg, I confess, I am a murderer. A murderer, Oleg. Oleg, embrace me, I am afraid.

OLEG. Now, now, Cleopatra Maximovna. Calm down.

CLEOPATRA. Oleg, you're not like the others. You're special. You won't judge me, will you? Oleg, I killed him.

OLEG. Who?

CLEOPATRA. Podsekalnikov. Oleg, he wanted my body. He wanted all of me, but I told him, "No!" And then he took his life because of me. Oleg, I am a murderer! I am afraid, Oleg. Take me home with you.

OLEG. I think you'd better go home alone, Cleopatra Maximovna.

CLEOPATRA. Oleg, I confess. My mother was a Gypsy. And her body simply drove men out of their minds. Ever since I was fifteen years old I've been her spitting image. I remember one time in Tiflis I went to buy some shoes and—would you believe it?—the salesman was so aroused by my beauty that he lost all control of himself. He bit my foot so hard I had to go to the hospital. Ever since then I have hated men. And then a foreigner fell in love with me. He wanted to deck me from head to foot in foreign clothes, but I told him, "No!" And then a communist fell head over heels in love with me. My God, how he worshipped me. He used to sit me on his knee and say, "Capochka, I'll give you the whole world. Let's go live in a village near Yalta." But I said, "No!" So he cursed me and resigned from the Communist Party. And then a pilot was seized by the desire to possess me. But I laughed in his face. He flew up over the city and cried up there in the sky until finally he crashed and killed himself. And now there's Podsekalnikov. Women fell before him like flies. Raisa was so consumed by passion that she started chewing glasses. She waited for him outside his door, but he wanted only me. He wanted my body, he wanted all of me, but I said, "No!" And then suddenly—poof!—he was gone. Since then I've begun hating my body. It frightens me. I can't remain in it. Oleg, take me home with you!

OLEG. Look, Cleopatra Maximovna, the fact of the matter is...

YELPIDY. (Off stage) Give unto him everlasting life!

CLEOPATRA. Oh my God, it's him. I feel sick. Hold me Oleg. Tighter. Tighter. Oleg, I'm getting weak. It's more than I can bear. Oleg, I don't have the strength to resist. I'm going to break loose at the burial. Oleg, you can't let me go. Tighter, hold me tighter. Let me go. Let me go. Oh, all right, I'll go.

OLEG. Where?

CLEOPATRA. With you to your house.

CHOIR. (Off stage) Eternal memory.

OLEG. Look, Cleopatra Maximovna. Only don't misunderstand what I'm trying to say. It's just that today is a little... well, inconvenient. You see...

CLEOPATRA. Say no more. I understand. Raisa is waiting for you at home. Oleg, let me open your eyes. Oleg, I swear to you on this grave here that Raisa is as phony as they come. Her whole body is built on deceit. Every morning she hooks her feet under the chest of drawers and does stomach exercises. But me? My mama was a Gypsy. I grew up a child of nature, with no false pretenses. Oleg, take me home with you.

OLEG. I assure you, Cleopatra Maximovna, today is a little inconvenient.

CHOIR. *(Off stage)* Eternal memory.

CLEOPATRA. In that case, Oleg Leonidovich, there's only one thing left for me to do. Farewell! *(She runs out)*

OLEG. Cleopatra Maximovna! Capa! Capochka! *(Runs after her)*

CHOIR. *(Off stage)* Eternal memory, eternal memory, eternal memory.

SCENE FIVE

(The coffin. A funeral procession. Father Yelpidy, the Deacon, the Choir, Mariya, Serafima, Margarita with the traditional bowl of rice, Aristarkh, Alexander, Viktor, Pugachyov, Yegor, Raisa, neighbors, streetwalkers, old women, couples out for a walk, curious passersby and torchbearers)

CHOIR. Eternal memory, eternal memory.

ARISTARKH. Careful, now. Careful.

ALEXANDER. Citizen, quit crowding the widow, please.

MARGARITA. Look out or you'll spill the rice.

YEGOR. Where do you think you're going?

FIRST OLD WOMAN. Let an old granny have a look, young man.

YEGOR. Are you the grandmother of the deceased?

FIRST OLD WOMAN. No, I'm just curious.

YEGOR. Then stand over here and look.

PUGACHYOV. Let me through.

ALEXANDER. There, it's in place now.

VIKTOR. Who will say a few words on behalf of the masses?

ARISTARKH. How about Yegor Timofeyevich?

VIKTOR. Well, say something, Yegor.

YEGOR. I'm afraid to.

ALEXANDER. What's there to fear, Yegor Timofeyevich? There's nothing terrible about a word of parting.

YEGOR. What do you mean a word isn't terrible? A word isn't a sparrow. Let it out and you'll never catch it again. See? You let it out, you don't catch it, and for that they catch you and don't let you out.

ARISTARKH. But you said you would.

YEGOR. I don't care. I still refuse. Anyway, I don't know how to begin.

VIKTOR. I have a wonderful beginning for you. Begin like this, Yegor

155

Timofeyevich: "There's something rotten in the state of Denmark."

YEGOR. Who said so?

VIKTOR. Marcellus.

YEGOR. Why didn't you say so before, you idiot? *(He runs to the mounds of dirt next to the grave)* Make way for the orator. *(Climbs up on a mound of dirt)* Citizens, allow me to share with you some joyous news. It has just come to our attention, thanks to comrade Marcellus, that the state of Denmark is rotting. I congratulate you. However, I can't say that this is unexpected. The rotting capitalist system has merely shown its true colors. Who's that tugging on me?

VIKTOR. What are you talking about? I gave you a lead, see? And then you were supposed to make a smooth transition and say something about the corpse.

YEGOR. Don't harass the orator. All right, here we go. And so, comrades, there's something rotten in Denmark, but right here among us, one of our own has passed away. But, shake it off, comrades, and let's all march forward in lock step with the corpse. And anyway, as I was saying about Denmark, comrades... Who's tugging on me again? Denmark is the...

(Aristarkh, Alexander and Viktor pull Yegor down from the mound of dirt)

VOICES. What happened? What's the problem?

ALEXANDER. Dear friends. The previous comrade suddenly took ill and can't go on. The wound is too fresh. The loss is too heavy. Tears of sorrow have welled in his throat.

MARIYA. Why go on living? Can anyone tell me that, citizens?

MARGARITA. Shh. Later, later, Mariya Lukyanovna. Don't interrupt the writer.

VIKTOR.

> Drink as you will, curse as you might,
> He paid for us the ultimate price.
> His life, in sum, resembled love.
> And ours is a pack of low lies.

> Oh, what a joy! Oh, what sweet splendor,
> To lie in the grass and roll in the snow.
> But, wherever I look, I see nothing but graves,
> Nothing but graves, wherever I go.

> Death is the answer for those without hope.
> It shines as a light from the heavens.
> But how many thousands have strayed from that path,
> Cowards, scoundrels and heathens?

He didn't waver. Yes, blood was his answer.
He paid for us the ultimate price.
His life, in sum, resembled love.
And ours is a pack of low lies.

RAISA. Quite nicely spoken.

YEGOR. Hey, comrades! I want to say something, too. Let me up there.

ALEXANDER. What do you want now? Grab him!

YEGOR. Keep your hands off me. *(Mounts the mound of dirt)* Now I will recite to you a poem about death, with a call to the masses for action. Mariya Lukyanovna, look over here and keep your eye on my hand. As soon as I wave my hand, you say, "who?" Got that? "Who?" All right. Here we go. My own personal poem about death, with a call to the masses for action.

VOICES IN THE CROWD. Shh. Shh.

YEGOR.
When once he lived, yes, lived among us,
And worked in a government office,
He was the best that anyone ever talked of... *(Waves his hand)*

MARIYA. *(Through tears)* Who?

YEGOR. Your husband, Semyon Podsekalnikov.

VIKTOR. Aristarkh Dominikovich, say something quick. Things are getting out of hand.

ARISTARKH. Senya has died. Semyon Podsekalnikov is no longer among us. I believe that the death of Podsekalnikov is the first alarm warning us about the pitiful plight of the Russian intelligentsia. It is only the first, mind you, comrades. As we all know, a single swallow spring does not make. Today it was he. Tomorrow, I shall be the one. Yes, comrades, tomorrow it will be I. Preserve the intelligentsia. I exhort you, comrades, preserve the intelligentsia. Raise your voices in its defense. Cry out in one voice, together...

SCENE SIX

(Cleopatra enters at a run with Oleg Leonidovich in hot pursuit)

OLEG. Capa! Capochka!

RAISA. Oleg!

OLEG. Raisa Filippovna!

CLEOPATRA. Let me through! Let me through to him!

VOICES. Who is that?

— What's the matter with her?

— She must be a relative.

— She must be mad!

CLEOPATRA. I come not to part with you, but to greet you.

VOICE IN THE CROWD. That's it. She's flipped her lid.

CLEOPATRA. It was for me that you took your life, and now I know what I must do.

VOICE IN THE CROWD. She sounds normal to me.

MARIYA. Excuse me, mademoiselle. Perhaps you've made a mistake. This was my husband.

CLEOPATRA. What do you know? He wanted my body. He wanted all of me. But I said, "No."

RAISA. She's lying. I'm the one who said, "No."

CLEOPATRA. He never even asked you.

RAISA. I suppose he asked you?

CLEOPATRA. He wanted my body.

RAISA. What's so interesting about your body?

ARISTARKH. Calm down. Calm down, comrades. This is not a personal tragedy, Raisa Filippovna. It is an alarm for society. Remember? Surrounded by mistrust and hostility, the Russian intelligentsia...

VIKTOR. Oh, knock it off. The corpse played the tuba. He was an artist. He burned, he wanted...

CLEOPATRA. He wanted my body. My body! My body!

PUGACHYOV. Meat, comrades. He wanted meat. Dear comrades, I am a butcher. But in our day and age, I am deprived of the right to do business. I haven't the strength. I have sworn. I have cursed. I even showed them all my ledgers. But no one has faith in the individual anymore, comrades. That's why people are shooting themselves.

YELPIDY. People have faith. They just don't have anywhere to practice their faith. All of the churches have been shut down.

PUGACHYOV. Who cares about churches when all of the stores have been shut down.

ARISTARKH. That's not why people shoot themselves. I was an intimate of the deceased. Ask his loved ones why he shot himself.

SERAFIMA. It was the liverwurst, Aristarkh Dominikovich.

PUGACHYOV. Liverwurst, exactly. Dear comrades, I am a butcher...

RAISA. That is base jealousy, Oleg Leonidovich. He shot himself for me.

CLEOPATRA. My body, my body...

YELPIDY. Religion...

PUGACHYOV. Meat...

ARISTARKH. Comrades...

PUGACHYOV. Liverwurst...

VIKTOR. Ideals...

ARISTARKH. The intelligentsia...

MARIYA. Senya! Senya!

SERAFIMA. You forgot about the corpse, citizens.

YELPIDY. May he know everlasting peace.

CHOIR. *(Sings)* Eternal memory, eternal memory.

(All kneel except Yegor. Viktor leaves)

MARGARITA. Why aren't you praying, Yegor Timofeyevich?

YEGOR. These days, praying is a sin.

YELPIDY. Let us bid farewell to the departed.

ARISTARKH. *(Kneeling)* Forgive me, Semyon. *(Kisses Podsekalnikov on the forehead)*

SEMYON. *(Embracing Aristarkh Dominikovich)* Forgive me, Aristarkh. *(Kisses him)*

ARISTARKH. Ah! *(Staggers back into the crowd)*

VOICES. Help!

SEMYON. *(Rising from the coffin)* Dear friends, please forgive me.

MARIYA. Senya! Senya!

SEMYON. Margarita Ivanovna! *(Runs to her)*

MARGARITA. *(Holding the bowl of rice)* Get thee from me, Satan! What do you want?

SEMYON. Rice, Margarita Ivanovna. Give me some rice. *(Grabs the bowl from her hands)* Comrades, I want to eat. *(Eats)* I lay here in this coffin for two nights and a day. And in all that time I was only able to sneak out to a bakery for a couple of bread rolls once. Comrades, I want to eat. But even more, I want to live.

ARISTARKH. How do you propose to do that?

SEMYON. However I can, but I want to live. When a chicken gets its head chopped off, it runs around with its head chopped off. I'll live like a chicken. I'll live like a chicken with its head chopped off. But I want to live. Comrades, I don't want to die. Not for you, not for them, not for society, not for humanity, not for Mariya Lukyanovna. You may be the dearest, most beloved, most wonderful people in my life. But in the face of death, nothing can be dearer or more beloved than my own hand, my leg, my stomach. I am in love with my stomach, comrades. I am madly in love with my stomach, comrades.

CLEOPATRA. Now this one is taking after Raisa Filippovna.

SEMYON. I am in love with my hands and feet, comrades. Oh, you marvelous, splendid little feet.

YELPIDY. What is wrong with him, Mariya Lukyanovna?

ARISTARKH. You are a scoundrel. You are a coward, citizen Podsekalnikov! What you have just said here is disgusting. Have you forgotten that the commonweal is always higher than the personal? That is the whole essence of every society.

159

SEMYON. What is society? Nothing but a conveyor belt of slogans. I'm not talking about a conveyor belt. I'm talking about a living human being. You keep using words: "commonweal," "personal." When they tell a man that war has been declared, what do you think the first thing is that comes into his head? Do you think this guy asks who the war is with? What it's being fought for? What ideals are being defended? No way. The first thing the poor guy asks is, "I wonder if they're drafting my age group?" And this guy is absolutely right.

ARISTARKH. What you are saying is that there are no heroes.

SEMYON. This world is big enough to hold anything, comrades. There are even women with beards. But I'm not talking about what might be. I'm talking about what is. And on this earth there is only one person who lives and fears death more than anything else in the world.

ALEXANDER. But you're the one who wanted to commit suicide.

ARISTARKH. You told us so yourself.

SEMYON. You're right. I did. Because the idea of suicide gave me something to live for. It brightened up my miserable, inhuman life, Aristarkh Dominikovich. Just think about it, comrades. Once upon a time there lived a man. And suddenly this man was made sub-human. Why? Do you really think I abandoned the human race? Do you really think I tried to avoid the October Revolution? I didn't leave my house once for the whole month of October. I have witnesses. I stand before you now as a man who was demoted to a cog. I have a word or two I'd like to say to this revolution. What more do you want of me? I gave you everything I had. I extended my hand to the revolution, my right hand. And you know what? Now my right hand votes against me. But what did the revolution give me? Nothing. And what about others? Look out on any street corner and you'll see what the revolution brought them. Why are you picking on me, comrades? When our government hangs out signs saying, "For everyone, for everyone," I don't pay any attention anymore. Because I know that means that everyone gets something except me. I'm not asking for much. You can have all your construction, your achievements, world conflagrations and conquests. All I want, comrades, is a peaceful little life and decent pay.

YELPIDY. What are you standing there staring for, Serafima Ilinishna? You're his mother-in-law. Make him shut up.

ALEXANDER. Stop him, comrades.

ARISTARKH. He's a counterrevolutionary.

SEMYON. God perish the thought. Do you really think we're doing something against the revolution? We haven't done a thing since the day it started. All we do is visit one another and talk about how hard life is. Because life is easier when we can say life is hard. For God's sake, don't deprive us of our last means of survival. Let us say that life is hard. Let us say it in a whisper, "Life is hard." Comrades, I implore you on behalf of millions of people: Give us the right to whisper. You'll be so busy constructing a new life that you'll never even hear us. I guarantee it. We'll live out our entire lives in a whisper.

PUGACHYOV. What's that supposed to mean? There's a rather strange turn of events, friends. I've held my silence long enough, good people. And now I'm going to have my say. You scum! You snake! You dug us a grave with your own hands and now you think you're going to live? Well, watch this then. I may kill myself doing it, but I'll have you shot, you thief. I'll have you shot.

RAISA. Shoot him!

VOICES. That's right!

SEMYON. Masha! Sweet Masha! Serafima Ilinishna! What are they saying? How can they? Forgive me. Why would you? Have mercy! What am I guilty of? I'll give you back everything you spent on me. I'll give it all back. Down to the last kopeck, you'll see. I'll sell my chest of drawers. If I have to, comrades, I'll quit eating. I'll make Mariya go to work for you and I'll send my mother-in-law into the mines. If you want me to, I'll go begging on the streets for you. Only let me live. (Gets down on his knees)

ARISTARKH. How utterly disgusting! Ugh!

SEMYON. (Leaping up) Who said, "ugh"? Whoever you are, step over here right now. (Takes out his pistol) Here's my pistol. Be my guest. Go on. Be my guest.

ARISTARKH. Quit playing games, Semyon Semyonovich. Put away your gun. Put away your gun, I tell you.

SEMYON. You don't have the guts. So what are you accusing me of, then? What crime did I commit? I just live my life. I live and I bother no one, comrades. I never harmed a soul. My whole life, I never hurt a flea. Let any man I've ever killed accuse me of it to my face.

(A funeral march)

SCENE SEVEN

(Enter Viktor at a run)

VIKTOR. Fedya Petunin shot himself. (Pause) And he left a suicide note.

ARISTARKH. What does it say?

VIKTOR. "Podsekalnikov is right. Life is not worth living."

(Funeral march)

THE END